The Ultimate Air Fryer

Cookbook for Beginners

1800 Days Foolproof 5-Ingredient Affordable Recipes for Healthy Eating Everyday

Francesca Giles

CONTENTS

Chapter 3 Bread And Breakfast Recipes 21

Chapter 4 Poultry Recipes 31

Chapter 7 Vegetarians Recipes 62

Chapter 8 Vegetable Side Dishes Recipes 71

INTRODUCTION

As technology develops each day, we can see so many new products that help us make cooking easier. On the other hand, thanks to technological benefits, people can prepare tastier food as well. One of the products that have experienced popularity growth in the last few years is definitely the air fryer.

What does it make so popular? The result of frying with nothing more than hot air. If you have already bought this fantastic appliance, I will share how you can use it, and all the other details you should know about it. Other than that, you will discover many tricks and tips that can make your cooking with an air fryer with a new experience.

The good news is that there are all kinds of food that you can air-fry. I have prepared a wide variety of different recipes with colorful pictures for you. On the other hand, if you still haven't purchased an air fryer yet, I am sure this book of recipes will change your way of thinking.

Let's go!

Chapter 1 Everything You Need to Know about Air Fryers

How the Air Fryers Work

The way air fryers work is easy to understand. Hot air circulates the food you placed there. As with any other cooking process, a chemical reaction called the Maillard effect manages the food's colorful look and flavor.

Heated air in the fryer comprises fine oil droplets that take the moisture out of the food. Interestingly, you don't need to put in a large amount of oil for a successful cooking process. You can use only one tablespoon, and you will get crispy traditional fried food that tastes delicious. As a result, you can have food that doesn't contain unhealthy fat and calories. Additionally, you will be pleasantly surprised to see the similarity of the fried food taste.

Step-by-Step Air Frying

1. Put your air fryer on a stable surface: For safety purposes, place your air fryer on a stable and heat-resistant surface. Moreover, make sure that there are at least five inches of space behind the air fryer for ventilation.

2. Spray oil on food: Most recipes designed for air fryers require a small amount of oil. Brushing oil on food can often lead to using more oil than necessary. Instead, use an oil spray bottle to conveniently coat your food with oil. There are many types of cooking oil that you can spray on your food but vegetable oil or olive oil always works for air fryers due to their high burning point.

3. Preheat the air fryer: Preheat the air fryer if recommended by your model. In general, preheating the air fryer requires only about 5 minutes but make sure to read your air fryer manual just to make sure that this step is indeed necessary or not.

4. Slice food into portions that will fit the air fryer: When cooking with the air fryer, make sure that you slice food into portions that will fit inside the fryer basket. Moreover, make sure that you do not overcrowd the air fryer basket. Creating spaces in between your food allows the air to properly circulate your food for even browning.

5. Use proper breading: When air frying food, make sure that you use the right breading. When breading your food, make sure that you coat it first with flour, eggs, and bread crumbs before misting or spraying it with cooking oil.

6. Always remember to monitor your food: In most cases, people tend to forget about this part. Monitoring your food by opening the fryer basket and checking halfway through the cooking time is important so that you don't burn your food. This is also crucial when you are cooking frozen foods.

7. Different food requires different cooking techniques: It is crucial to take note that different kinds of foods require different cooking techniques in your air fryer. For instance, vegetables needed to be shaken vigorously or halfway through the cooking time.

8. Always start with a clean air fryer: When cooking foods that are naturally greasy, make sure that you start with a clean air fryer. Remove any oil that has been stuck at the bottom of the air fryer. During the cooking process, make sure that you also empty the frying basket oi oil halfway through the cooking time as excess oil can cause too much smoke that can even burn your food.

9. Create an aluminum sling: Getting your air fryer accessories in and out of the air fryer basket can be difficult especially when the air fryer is hot. To facilitate the transfer, you can use a long aluminum foil folded into a sling and placing it at the bottom of the baking dish so that you can easily lift it once the cooking time ends.

Air Fryer Tips & Tricks

1. Preheat the air fryer before placing the food inside.

Even when you are going to cook food in the oven, you preheat it for a few minutes before placing the food inside. The process is the same with an air fryer. The taste of food will be more delicious in the preheated conditions. Despite that, this is a simple step that many people forget. For that reason, keep in mind the importance of remembering this advice.

2. Add spices to the oil before spreading them over the food.

Many people don't know that the air circulation in this machine is very strong. That's why some lightweight spices can be blow off. If you want to prevent that, do as the title says, and mix some spices with oil. The oil will hold the spices and herbs on the food.

3. **Avoid using nonstick aerosol spray to prevent damaging your air fryer.**

Many people don't know that nonstick cooking sprays can include additives. Those additives can produce damage to the non-sticking layer of your machine. For that reason, remember to avoid them. However, there is a perfect alternative you can find. You can buy a spray bottle and pour your oil into it.

4. **Leave at least five inches of space around your air fryer.**

You need to leave enough space around all sides of your air fryer if you want to provide adequate air circulation. There is a rule of thumb to provide five inches of space around the fryer and check that the surface is heat-proof.

5. **Don't overcrowd your air fryer.**

If you add too many foods into your air fryer basket, you will cause a big problem. The air fryer cannot work properly when it is overcrowded. The air circulation will be disrupted, and the food won't taste delicious. If you need to prepare a large amount of food, you need to cook it in small air fryer batches. This way, you will ensure that your food gets crispy. Keep in mind to follow this advice, especially when you are making fries.

Caring for Your Air Fryer

You don't have to invest in any specific detergent or cleanser to keep your air fryer smelling like new. Use this section as your guide to keep your new kitchen appliance in tip-top shape so you can use it for years to come.

Cleaning your air fryer

Cleaning your air fryer is actually a really simple task. With a little elbow grease, some regular dish detergent, and hot water, your air fryer will come back to life, even with the toughest of buildup.

We've experimented with various makes and models and had our fair share of epic disasters in our air fryers (think: cream cheese melted with panko all over the baking tray), but guess what? After letting the basket and/or tray cool, we were easily able to get the buildup off with a regular kitchen sponge and hot soapy water.

Plus, even when switching between seafood and a decadent dessert, the air fryer doesn't require a deep clean.

Wipe down the outside of your fryer after each use. A hot, soapy towel is all that's necessary. This helps get off any grease or food particles that may have latched on during cooking.

Storing your air fryer

You can purchase a snazzy air fryer cover online, but this isn't necessary. We store our air fryers on the countertop because, well, we're writing a cookbook and we use them more frequently! Unfortunately, many models are too bulky for under-the-counter storage. Wherever you choose to store your air fryer, just be sure to put it in an area of your kitchen that isn't near your stovetop or oven so you don't get the residual grease from your day-to-day cooking building up on the outside of it.

BASIC KITCHEN CONVERSIONS & EQUIVALENTS

DRY MEASUREMENTS CONVERSION CHART

3 TEASPOONS = 1 TABLESPOON = 1/16 CUP

6 TEASPOONS = 2 TABLESPOONS = 1/8 CUP

12 TEASPOONS = 4 TABLESPOONS = 1/4 CUP

24 TEASPOONS = 8 TABLESPOONS = 1/2 CUP

36 TEASPOONS = 12 TABLESPOONS = 3/4 CUP

48 TEASPOONS = 16 TABLESPOONS = 1 CUP

METRIC TO US COOKING CONVERSIONS

OVEN TEMPERATURES

120 °C = 250 °F

160 °C = 320 °F

180° C = 350 °F

205 °C = 400 °F

220 °C = 425 °F

LIQUID MEASUREMENTS CONVERSION CHART

8 FLUID OUNCES = 1 CUP = 1/2 PINT = 1/4 QUART

16 FLUID OUNCES = 2 CUPS = 1 PINT = 1/2 QUART

32 FLUID OUNCES = 4 CUPS = 2 PINTS = 1 QUART = 1/4 GALLON

128 FLUID OUNCES = 16 CUPS = 8 PINTS = 4 QUARTS = 1 GALLON

BAKING IN GRAMS

1 CUP FLOUR = 140 GRAMS

1 CUP SUGAR = 150 GRAMS

1 CUP POWDERED SUGAR = 160 GRAMS

1 CUP HEAVY CREAM = 235 GRAMS

VOLUME

1 MILLILITER = 1/5 TEASPOON

5 ML = 1 TEASPOON

15 ML = 1 TABLESPOON

240 ML = 1 CUP OR 8 FLUID OUNCES

1 LITER = 34 FL. OUNCES

WEIGHT

1 GRAM = .035 OUNCES

100 GRAMS = 3.5 OUNCES

500 GRAMS = 1.1 POUNDS

1 KILOGRAM = 35 OUNCES

US TO METRIC COOKING CONVERSIONS

1/5 TSP = 1 ML

1 TSP = 5 ML

1 TBSP = 15 ML

1 FL OUNCE = 30 ML

1 CUP = 237 ML

1 PINT (2 CUPS) = 473 ML

1 QUART (4 CUPS) = .95 LITER

1 GALLON (16 CUPS) = 3.8 LITERS

1 OZ = 28 GRAMS

1 POUND = 454 GRAMS

BUTTER

1 CUP BUTTER = 2 STICKS = 8 OUNCES = 230 GRAMS = 8 TABLESPOONS

WHAT DOES 1 CUP EQUAL

1 CUP = 8 FLUID OUNCES

1 CUP = 16 TABLESPOONS

1 CUP = 48 TEASPOONS

1 CUP = 1/2 PINT

1 CUP = 1/4 QUART

1 CUP = 1/16 GALLON

1 CUP = 240 ML

BAKING PAN CONVERSIONS

1 CUP ALL-PURPOSE FLOUR = 4.5 OZ

1 CUP ROLLED OATS = 3 OZ 1 LARGE EGG = 1.7 OZ

1 CUP BUTTER = 8 OZ 1 CUP MILK = 8 OZ

1 CUP HEAVY CREAM = 8.4 OZ

1 CUP GRANULATED SUGAR = 7.1 OZ

1 CUP PACKED BROWN SUGAR = 7.75 OZ

1 CUP VEGETABLE OIL = 7.7 OZ

1 CUP UNSIFTED POWDERED SUGAR = 4.4 OZ

BAKING PAN CONVERSIONS

9-INCH ROUND CAKE PAN = 12 CUPS

10-INCH TUBE PAN =16 CUPS

11-INCH BUNDT PAN = 12 CUPS

9-INCH SPRINGFORM PAN = 10 CUPS

9 X 5 INCH LOAF PAN = 8 CUPS

9-INCH SQUARE PAN = 8 CUPS

Chapter 2 Appetizers And Snacks Recipes

Chapter 2 Appetizers And Snacks Recipes

Spicy Sweet Potato Tater-tots

Servings: 6 | Cooking Time: 10 Minutes

Ingredients:

- 6 cups filtered water
- 2 medium sweet potatoes, peeled and cut in half
- 1 teaspoon garlic powder
- ½ teaspoon black pepper, divided
- ½ teaspoon salt, divided
- 1 cup panko breadcrumbs
- 1 teaspoon blackened seasoning

Directions:

1. In a large stovetop pot, bring the water to a boil. Add the sweet potatoes and let boil about 10 minutes, until a metal fork prong can be inserted but the potatoes still have a slight give.
2. Carefully remove the potatoes from the pot and let cool.
3. When you're able to touch them, grate the potatoes into a large bowl. Mix the garlic powder, ¼ teaspoon of the black pepper, and ¼ teaspoon of the salt into the potatoes. Place the mixture in the refrigerator and let set at least 45 minutes.
4. Before assembling, mix the breadcrumbs and blackened seasoning in a small bowl.
5. Remove the sweet potatoes from the refrigerator and preheat the air fryer to 400°F.
6. Assemble the tater-tots by using a teaspoon to portion batter evenly and form into a tater-tot shape. Roll each tater-tot in the breadcrumb mixture. Then carefully place the tater-tots in the air fryer basket. Be sure that you've liberally sprayed the air fryer basket with an olive oil mist. Repeat until tater-tots fill the basket without touching one another. You'll need to do multiple batches, depending on the size of your air fryer.
7. Cook the tater-tots for 3 to 6 minutes, flip, and cook another 3 to 6 minutes.
8. Remove from the air fryer carefully and keep warm until ready to serve.

Sweet And Spicy Beef Jerky

Servings:6 | Cooking Time: 4 Hours

Ingredients:

- 1 pound eye of round beef, fat trimmed, sliced into ¼"-thick strips
- ¼ cup soy sauce
- 2 tablespoons sriracha hot chili sauce
- ½ teaspoon ground black pepper
- 2 tablespoons granular brown erythritol

Directions:

1. Place beef in a large sealable bowl or bag. Pour soy sauce and sriracha into bowl or bag, then sprinkle in pepper and erythritol. Shake or stir to combine ingredients and coat steak. Cover and place in refrigerator to marinate at least 2 hours up to overnight.
2. Once marinated, remove strips from marinade and pat dry. Place into ungreased air fryer basket in a single layer, working in batches if needed. Adjust the temperature to 180°F and set the timer for 4 hours. Jerky will be chewy and dark brown when done. Store in airtight container in a cool, dry place up to 2 weeks.

Buffalo French Fries

Servings: 6 | Cooking Time: 35 Minutes

Ingredients:

- 3 large russet potatoes
- 2 tbsp buffalo sauce
- 2 tbsp extra-virgin olive oil
- Salt and pepper to taste

Directions:

1. Preheat air fryer to 380°F. Peel and cut potatoes lengthwise into French fries. Place them in a bowl, then coat with olive oil, salt and pepper. Air Fry them for 10 minutes. Shake the basket, then cook for five minutes. Serve drizzled with Buffalo sauce immediately.

Mini Greek Meatballs

Servings:36 | Cooking Time: 10 Minutes

Ingredients:

- 1 cup fresh spinach leaves
- ¼ cup peeled and diced red onion
- ½ cup crumbled feta cheese
- 1 pound 85/15 ground turkey
- ½ teaspoon salt
- ½ teaspoon ground cumin
- ¼ teaspoon ground black pepper

Directions:

1. Place spinach, onion, and feta in a food processor, and pulse ten times until spinach is chopped. Scoop into a large bowl.
2. Add turkey to bowl and sprinkle with salt, cumin, and pepper. Mix until fully combined. Roll mixture into thirty-six meatballs.
3. Place meatballs into ungreased air fryer basket, working in batches if needed. Adjust the temperature to 350°F and set the timer for 10 minutes, shaking basket twice during cooking. Meatballs will be browned and have an internal temperature of at least 165°F when done. Serve warm.

Bacon-wrapped Cabbage Bites

Servings:6 | Cooking Time: 12 Minutes

Ingredients:

- 3 tablespoons sriracha hot chili sauce, divided
- 1 medium head cabbage, cored and cut into 12 bite-sized pieces
- 2 tablespoons coconut oil, melted
- ½ teaspoon salt
- 12 slices sugar-free bacon
- ½ cup mayonnaise
- ¼ teaspoon garlic powder

Directions:

1. Evenly brush 2 tablespoons sriracha onto cabbage pieces. Drizzle evenly with coconut oil, then sprinkle with salt.
2. Wrap each cabbage piece with bacon and secure with a toothpick. Place into ungreased air fryer basket. Adjust the temperature to 375°F and set the timer for 12 minutes, turning cabbage halfway through cooking. Bacon will be cooked and crispy when done.
3. In a small bowl, whisk together mayonnaise, garlic powder, and remaining sriracha. Use as a dipping sauce for cabbage bites.

Bacon-wrapped Mozzarella Sticks

Servings:6 | Cooking Time: 12 Minutes

Ingredients:

- 6 sticks mozzarella string cheese
- 6 slices sugar-free bacon

Directions:

1. Place mozzarella sticks on a medium plate, cover, and place into freezer 1 hour until frozen solid.
2. Wrap each mozzarella stick in 1 piece of bacon and secure with a toothpick. Place into ungreased air fryer basket. Adjust the temperature to 400°F and set the timer for 12 minutes, turning sticks once during cooking. Bacon will be crispy when done. Serve warm.

Beer-battered Onion Rings

Servings: 4 | Cooking Time: 25 Minutes

Ingredients:

- 2 sliced onions, rings separated
- 1 cup flour
- Salt and pepper to taste
- 1 tsp garlic powder
- 1 cup beer

Directions:

1. Preheat air fryer to 350°F. In a mixing bowl, combine the flour, garlic powder, beer, salt, and black pepper. Dip the onion rings into the bowl and lay the coated rings in the frying basket. Air Fry for 15 minutes, shaking the basket several times during cooking to jostle the onion rings and ensure a good even fry. Once ready, the onions should be crispy and golden brown. Serve hot.

Okra Chips

Servings: 4 | Cooking Time: 16 Minutes

Ingredients:

- 1¼ pounds Thin fresh okra pods, cut into 1-inch pieces
- 1½ tablespoons Vegetable or canola oil
- ¾ teaspoon Coarse sea salt or kosher salt

Directions:

1. Preheat the air fryer to 400°F.
2. Toss the okra, oil, and salt in a large bowl until the pieces are well and evenly coated.
3. When the machine is at temperature, pour the contents of the bowl into the basket. Air-fry, tossing several times, for 16 minutes, or until crisp and quite brown.
4. Pour the contents of the basket onto a wire rack. Cool for a couple of minutes before serving.

Baba Ghanouj

Servings: 2 | Cooking Time: 40 Minutes

Ingredients:

- 2 Small purple Italian eggplant(s)
- ¼ cup Olive oil
- ¼ cup Tahini
- ½ teaspoon Ground black pepper
- ¼ teaspoon Onion powder
- ¼ teaspoon Mild smoked paprika (optional)
- Up to 1 teaspoon Table salt

Directions:

1. Preheat the air fryer to 400°F.
2. Prick the eggplant(s) on all sides with a fork. When the machine is at temperature, set the eggplant(s) in the basket in one layer. Air-fry undisturbed for 40 minutes, or until blackened and soft.
3. Remove the basket from the machine. Cool the eggplant(s) in the basket for 20 minutes.
4. Use a nonstick-safe spatula, and perhaps a flatware tablespoon for balance, to gently transfer the eggplant(s) to a bowl. The juices will run out. Make sure the bowl is close to the basket. Split the eggplant(s) open.
5. Scrape the soft insides of half an eggplant into a food processor. Repeat with the remaining piece(s). Add any juices from the bowl to the eggplant in the food processor, but discard the skins and stems.
6. Add the olive oil, tahini, pepper, onion powder, and smoked paprika. Add about half the salt, then cover and process until smooth, stopping the machine at least once to scrape down the inside of the canister. Check the spread for salt and add more as needed. Scrape the baba ghanouj into a bowl and serve warm, or set aside at room temperature for up to 2 hours, or cover and store in the refrigerator for up to 4 days.

Easy Crispy Prawns

Servings:4 | Cooking Time:10 Minutes

Ingredients:

- 1 egg
- ½ pound nacho chips, crushed
- 18 prawns, peeled and deveined
- Salt and black pepper, to taste

Directions:

1. Preheat the Air fryer to 355°F and grease an Air fryer basket.
2. Crack egg in a shallow dish and beat well.
3. Place the crushed nacho chips in another shallow dish.
4. Coat prawns into egg and then roll into nacho chips.
5. Place the coated prawns into the Air fryer basket and cook for about 10 minutes.
6. Dish out and serve warm.

Home-style Taro Chips

Servings: 2 | Cooking Time: 20 Minutes

Ingredients:

- 1 tbsp olive oil
- 1 cup thinly sliced taro
- Salt to taste
- ½ cup hummus

Directions:

1. Preheat air fryer to 325°F. Put the sliced taro in the greased frying basket, spread the pieces out, and drizzle with olive oil. Air Fry for 10-12 minutes, shaking the basket twice. Sprinkle with salt and serve with hummus.

Italian Bruschetta With Mushrooms & Cheese

Servings: 4 | Cooking Time: 25 Minutes

Ingredients:

- ½ cup button mushrooms, chopped
- ½ baguette, sliced
- 1 garlic clove, minced
- 3 oz sliced Parmesan cheese
- 1 tbsp extra virgin olive oil
- Salt and pepper to taste

Directions:

1. Preheat air fryer to 350°F. Add the mushrooms, olive oil, salt, pepper, and garlic to a mixing bowl and stir thoroughly to combine. Divide the mushroom mixture between the bread slices, drizzling all over the surface with olive oil, then cover with Parmesan slices. Place the covered bread slices in the greased frying basket and Bake for 15 minutes. Serve and enjoy!

Homemade Pretzel Bites

Servings: 8 | Cooking Time: 6 Minutes

Ingredients:
- 4¾ cups filtered water, divided
- 1 tablespoon butter
- 1 package fast-rising yeast
- ½ teaspoon salt
- 2⅓ cups bread flour
- 2 tablespoons baking soda
- 2 egg whites
- 1 teaspoon kosher salt

Directions:
1. Preheat the air fryer to 370°F.
2. In a large microwave-safe bowl, add ¾ cup of the water. Heat for 40 seconds in the microwave. Remove and whisk in the butter; then mix in the yeast and salt. Let sit 5 minutes.
3. Using a stand mixer with a dough hook attachment, add the yeast liquid and mix in the bread flour ⅓ cup at a time until all the flour is added and a dough is formed.
4. Remove the bowl from the stand; then let the dough rise 1 hour in a warm space, covered with a kitchen towel.
5. After the dough has doubled in size, remove from the bowl and punch down a few times on a lightly floured flat surface.
6. Divide the dough into 4 balls; then roll each ball out into a long, skinny, sticklike shape. Using a sharp knife, cut each dough stick into 6 pieces.
7. Repeat Step 6 for the remaining dough balls until you have about 24 bites formed.
8. Heat the remaining 4 cups of water over the stovetop in a medium pot with the baking soda stirred in.
9. Drop the pretzel bite dough into the hot water and let boil for 60 seconds, remove, and let slightly cool.
10. Lightly brush the top of each bite with the egg whites, and then cover with a pinch of kosher salt.
11. Spray the air fryer basket with olive oil spray and place the pretzel bites on top. Cook for 6 to 8 minutes, or until lightly browned. Remove and keep warm.
12. Repeat until all pretzel bites are cooked.
13. Serve warm.

Bacon, Sausage And Bell Pepper Skewers

Servings: 4 | Cooking Time: 20 Minutes

Ingredients:
- 16 cocktail sausages, halved
- 4 ounces bacon, diced
- 1 red bell pepper, cut into 1 ½-inch pieces
- 1 green bell pepper, cut into 1 ½-inch pieces
- Salt and cracked black pepper, to taste
- 1/2 cup tomato chili sauce

Directions:
1. Thread the cocktail sausages, bacon, and peppers alternately onto skewers. Sprinkle with salt and black pepper.
2. Cook in the preheated Air Fryer at 380°F for 15 minutes, turning the skewers over once or twice to ensure even cooking.
3. Serve with the tomato chili sauce on the side. Enjoy!

Buffalo Cauliflower Wings

Servings:4 | Cooking Time: 14 Minutes

Ingredients:

- 1 cauliflower head, cut into florets
- 1 tbsp butter, melted
- 1/2 cup buffalo sauce
- Pepper
- Salt

Directions:

1. Spray air fryer basket with cooking spray.
2. In a bowl, mix together buffalo sauce, butter, pepper, and salt.
3. Add cauliflower florets into the air fryer basket and cook at 400 °F for 7 minutes.
4. Transfer cauliflower florets into the buffalo sauce mixture and toss well.
5. Again, add cauliflower florets into the air fryer basket and cook for 7 minutes more at 400 °F.
6. Serve and enjoy.

Crispy Salami Roll-ups

Servings:16 | Cooking Time: 4 Minutes

Ingredients:

- 4 ounces cream cheese, broken into 16 equal pieces
- 16 deli slices Genoa salami

Directions:

1. Place a piece of cream cheese at the edge of a slice of salami and roll to close. Secure with a toothpick. Repeat with remaining cream cheese pieces and salami.
2. Place roll-ups in an ungreased 6" round nonstick baking dish and place into air fryer basket. Adjust the temperature to 350°F and set the timer for 4 minutes. Salami will be crispy and cream cheese will be warm when done. Let cool 5 minutes before serving.

Rumaki

Servings: 24 | Cooking Time: 12 Minutes

Ingredients:

- 10 ounces raw chicken livers
- 1 can sliced water chestnuts, drained
- ¼ cup low-sodium teriyaki sauce
- 12 slices turkey bacon
- toothpicks

Directions:

1. Cut livers into 1½-inch pieces, trimming out tough veins as you slice.
2. Place livers, water chestnuts, and teriyaki sauce in small container with lid. If needed, add another tablespoon of teriyaki sauce to make sure livers are covered. Refrigerate for 1 hour.
3. When ready to cook, cut bacon slices in half crosswise.
4. Wrap 1 piece of liver and 1 slice of water chestnut in each bacon strip. Secure with toothpick.
5. When you have wrapped half of the livers, place them in the air fryer basket in a single layer.
6. Cook at 390°F for 12 minutes, until liver is done and bacon is crispy.
7. While first batch cooks, wrap the remaining livers. Repeat step 6 to cook your second batch.

Bacon-wrapped Goat Cheese Poppers

Servings: 10 | Cooking Time: 10 Minutes

Ingredients:

- 10 large jalapeño peppers
- 8 ounces goat cheese
- 10 slices bacon

Directions:

1. Preheat the air fryer to 380°F.
2. Slice the jalapeños in half. Carefully remove the veins and seeds of the jalapeños with a spoon.
3. Fill each jalapeño half with 2 teaspoons goat cheese.
4. Cut the bacon in half lengthwise to make long strips. Wrap the jalapeños with bacon, trying to cover the entire length of the jalapeño.
5. Place the bacon-wrapped jalapeños into the air fryer basket. Cook the stuffed jalapeños for 10 minutes or until bacon is crispy.

Crispy Prawns

Servings:4 | Cooking Time: 8 Minutes

Ingredients:

- 1 egg
- ½ pound nacho chips, crushed
- 18 prawns, peeled and deveined

Directions:

1. In a shallow dish, crack the egg, and beat well.
2. Put the crushed nacho chips in another dish.
3. Now, dip the prawn into beaten egg and then, coat with the nacho chips.
4. Set the temperature of Air Fryer to 355°F.
5. Place the prawns in an Air Fryer basket in a single layer.
6. Air Fry for about 8 minutes.
7. Serve hot.

Italian Dip

Servings:8 | Cooking Time: 12 Minutes

Ingredients:

- 8 oz cream cheese, softened
- 1 cup mozzarella cheese, shredded
- 1/2 cup roasted red peppers
- 1/3 cup basil pesto
- 1/4 cup parmesan cheese, grated

Directions:

1. Add parmesan cheese and cream cheese into the food processor and process until smooth.
2. Transfer cheese mixture into the air fryer pan and spread evenly.
3. Pour basil pesto on top of cheese layer.
4. Sprinkle roasted pepper on top of basil pesto layer.
5. Sprinkle mozzarella cheese on top of pepper layer and place dish in air fryer basket.
6. Cook dip at 250°F for 12 minutes.
7. Serve and enjoy.

Chapter 3 Bread And Breakfast Recipes

Chapter 3 Bread And Breakfast Recipes

Very Berry Breakfast Puffs

Servings:3 | Cooking Time: 20 Minutes

Ingredients:
- 2 tbsp mashed strawberries
- 2 tbsp mashed raspberries
- ¼ tsp vanilla extract
- 2 cups cream cheese
- 1 tbsp honey

Directions:

1. Preheat the air fryer to 375°F. Divide the cream cheese between the dough sheets and spread it evenly. In a small bowl, combine the berries, honey and vanilla.

2. Divide the mixture between the pastry sheets. Pinch the ends of the sheets, to form puff. Place the puffs on a lined baking dish. Place the dish in the air fryer and cook for 15 minutes.

Roasted Golden Mini Potatoes

Servings:4 | Cooking Time: 22 Minutes

Ingredients:
- 6 cups water
- 1 pound baby Dutch yellow potatoes, quartered
- 2 tablespoons olive oil
- ½ teaspoon garlic powder
- ¾ teaspoon seasoned salt
- ¼ teaspoon salt
- ½ teaspoon ground black pepper

Directions:

1. In a medium saucepan over medium-high heat bring water to a boil. Add potatoes and boil 10 minutes until fork-tender, then drain and gently pat dry.

2. Preheat the air fryer to 400°F.

3. Drizzle oil over potatoes, then sprinkle with garlic powder, seasoned salt, salt, and pepper.

4. Place potatoes in the air fryer basket and cook 12 minutes, shaking the basket three times during cooking. Potatoes will be done when golden brown and edges are crisp. Serve warm.

Grilled Steak With Parsley Salad

Servings:4 | Cooking Time: 45 Minutes

Ingredients:

- 1 ½ pounds flatiron steak
- 3 tablespoons olive oil
- Salt and pepper to taste
- 2 cups parsley leaves
- ½ cup parmesan cheese, grated
- 1 tablespoon fresh lemon juice

Directions:

1. Preheat the air fryer at 390°F.
2. Place the grill pan accessory in the air fryer.
3. Mix together the steak, oil, salt and pepper.
4. Grill for 15 minutes per batch and make sure to flip the meat halfway through the cooking time.
5. Meanwhile, prepare the salad by combining in a bowl the parsley leaves, parmesan cheese and lemon juice. Season with salt and pepper.

Bacon Cups

Servings: 2 | Cooking Time: 40 Minutes

Ingredients:

- 2 eggs
- 1 slice tomato
- 3 slices bacon
- 2 slices ham
- 2 tsp grated parmesan cheese

Directions:

1. Preheat your fryer to 375°F
2. Cook the bacon for half of the directed time.
3. Slice the bacon strips in half and line 2 greased muffin tins with 3 half-strips of bacon
4. Put one slice of ham and half slice of tomato in each muffin tin on top of the bacon
5. Crack one egg on top of the tomato in each muffin tin and sprinkle each with half a teaspoon of grated parmesan cheese.
6. Bake for 20 minutes.
7. Remove and let cool.
8. Serve!

Scrambled Eggs

Servings: 2 | Cooking Time: 6 Minutes

Ingredients:

- 4 eggs
- 1/4 tsp garlic powder
- 1/4 tsp onion powder
- 1 tbsp parmesan cheese
- Pepper
- Salt

Directions:

1. Whisk eggs with garlic powder, onion powder, parmesan cheese, pepper, and salt.
2. Pour egg mixture into the air fryer baking dish.
3. Place dish in the air fryer and cook at 360°F for 2 minutes. Stir quickly and cook for 3-4 minutes more.
4. Stir well and serve.

Pancake For Two

Servings:2 | Cooking Time: 30 Minutes

Ingredients:

- 1 cup blanched finely ground almond flour
- 2 tablespoons granular erythritol
- 1 tablespoon salted butter, melted
- 1 large egg
- ⅓ cup unsweetened almond milk
- ½ teaspoon vanilla extract

Directions:

1. In a large bowl, mix all ingredients together, then pour half the batter into an ungreased 6" round nonstick baking dish.
2. Place dish into air fryer basket. Adjust the temperature to 320°F and set the timer for 15 minutes. The pancake will be golden brown on top and firm, and a toothpick inserted in the center will come out clean when done. Repeat with remaining batter.
3. Slice in half in dish and serve warm.

Cream Cheese Danish

Servings:4 | Cooking Time: 10 Minutes

Ingredients:
- 1 sheet frozen puff pastry dough, thawed
- 1 large egg, beaten
- 4 ounces full-fat cream cheese, softened
- ¼ cup confectioners' sugar
- 1 teaspoon vanilla extract
- ½ teaspoon lemon juice

Directions:
1. Preheat the air fryer to 320°F.
2. Unfold puff pastry and cut into four equal squares. For each pastry, fold all four corners partway to the center, leaving a 1" square in the center.
3. Brush egg evenly over folded puff pastry.
4. In a medium bowl, mix cream cheese, confectioners' sugar, vanilla, and lemon juice. Scoop 2 tablespoons of mixture into the center of each pastry square.
5. Place danishes directly in the air fryer basket and cook 10 minutes until puffy and golden brown. Cool 5 minutes before serving.

Bacon Puff Pastry Pinwheels

Servings: 8 | Cooking Time: 10 Minutes

Ingredients:
- 1 sheet of puff pastry
- 2 tablespoons maple syrup
- ¼ cup brown sugar
- 8 slices bacon (not thick cut)
- coarsely cracked black pepper
- vegetable oil

Directions:
1. On a lightly floured surface, roll the puff pastry out into a square that measures roughly 10 inches wide by however long your bacon strips are. Cut the pastry into eight even strips.
2. Brush the strips of pastry with the maple syrup and sprinkle the brown sugar on top, leaving 1 inch of dough exposed at the far end of each strip. Place a slice of bacon on each strip of puff pastry, letting 1/8-inch of the length of bacon hang over the edge of the pastry. Season generously with coarsely ground black pepper.
3. With the exposed end of the pastry strips away from you, roll the bacon and pastry strips up into pinwheels. Dab a little water on the exposed end of the pastry and pinch it to the pinwheel to seal the pastry shut.
4. Preheat the air fryer to 360°F.
5. Brush or spray the air fryer basket with a little vegetable oil. Place the pinwheels into the basket and air-fry at 360°F for 8 minutes. Turn the pinwheels over and air-fry for another 2 minutes to brown the bottom. Serve warm.

Onion Marinated Skirt Steak

Servings:3 | Cooking Time: 45 Minutes

Ingredients:

- 1 large red onion, grated or pureed
- 2 tablespoons brown sugar
- 1 tablespoon vinegar
- 1 ½ pounds skirt steak
- Salt and pepper to taste

Directions:

1. Place all ingredients in a Ziploc bag and allow to marinate in the fridge for at least 2 hours.
2. Preheat the air fryer at 390°F.
3. Place the grill pan accessory in the air fryer.
4. Grill for 15 minutes per batch.
5. Flip every 8 minutes for even grilling.

Hashbrown Potatoes Lyonnaise

Servings: 4 | Cooking Time: 33 Minutes

Ingredients:

- 1 Vidalia (or other sweet) onion, sliced
- 1 teaspoon butter, melted
- 1 teaspoon brown sugar
- 2 large russet potatoes, sliced ½-inch thick
- 1 tablespoon vegetable oil
- salt and freshly ground black pepper

Directions:

1. Preheat the air fryer to 370°F.
2. Toss the sliced onions, melted butter and brown sugar together in the air fryer basket. Air-fry for 8 minutes, shaking the basket occasionally to help the onions cook evenly.
3. While the onions are cooking, bring a 3-quart saucepan of salted water to a boil on the stovetop. Par-cook the potatoes in boiling water for 3 minutes. Drain the potatoes and pat them dry with a clean kitchen towel.
4. Add the potatoes to the onions in the air fryer basket and drizzle with vegetable oil. Toss to coat the potatoes with the oil and season with salt and freshly ground black pepper.
5. Increase the air fryer temperature to 400°F and air-fry for 22 minutes tossing the vegetables a few times during the cooking time to help the potatoes brown evenly. Season to taste again with salt and freshly ground black pepper and serve warm.

Tri-color Frittata

Servings: 4 | Cooking Time: 30 Minutes

Ingredients:

- 8 eggs, beaten
- 1 red bell pepper, diced
- Salt and pepper to taste
- 1 garlic clove, minced
- ½ tsp dried oregano
- ½ cup ricotta

Directions:

1. Preheat air fryer to 360°F. Place the beaten eggs, bell pepper, oregano, salt, black pepper, and garlic and mix well. Fold in ¼ cup half of ricotta cheese.
2. Pour the egg mixture into a greased cake pan and top with the remaining ricotta. Place into the air fryer and Bake for 18-20 minutes or until the eggs are set in the center. Let the frittata cool for 5 minutes. Serve sliced.

Hash Browns

Servings:2 | Cooking Time: 30 Minutes

Ingredients:

- 2 large russet potatoes, peeled
- 2 cups cold water
- 1 tablespoon olive oil
- ½ teaspoon salt

Directions:

1. Grate potatoes into a bowl filled with cold water. Let soak 10 minutes. Drain into a colander, then press into paper towels to remove excess moisture.
2. Dry the bowl and return potatoes to it. Toss with oil and salt.
3. Preheat the air fryer to 375°F. Spray a 6" round cake pan with cooking spray.
4. Pour potatoes into prepared pan, pressing them down.
5. Cook 20 minutes until brown and crispy. Serve warm.

Mushrooms Spread

Servings: 4 | Cooking Time: 20 Minutes

Ingredients:

- 1 cup white mushrooms
- ¼ cup mozzarella, shredded
- ½ cup coconut cream
- A pinch of salt and black pepper
- Cooking spray

Directions:

1. Put the mushrooms in your air fryer's basket, grease with cooking spray and cook at 370°F for 20 minutes. Transfer to a blender, add the remaining ingredients, pulse well, divide into bowls and serve as a spread.

Parsley Omelet

Servings: 4 | Cooking Time: 15 Minutes

Ingredients:

- 4 eggs, whisked
- 1 tablespoon parsley, chopped
- ½ teaspoons cheddar cheese, shredded
- 1 avocado, peeled, pitted and cubed
- Cooking spray

Directions:

1. In a bowl, mix all the ingredients except the cooking spray and whisk well. Grease a baking pan that fits the Air Fryer with the cooking spray, pour the omelet mix, spread, introduce the pan in the machine and cook at 370°F for 15 minutes. Serve for breakfast.

Seasoned Herbed Sourdough Croutons

Servings: 4 | Cooking Time: 7 Minutes

Ingredients:

- 4 cups cubed sourdough bread, 1-inch cubes
- 1 tablespoon olive oil
- 1 teaspoon fresh thyme leaves
- ¼ – ½ teaspoon salt
- freshly ground black pepper

Directions:

1. Combine all ingredients in a bowl and taste to make sure it is seasoned to your liking.
2. Preheat the air fryer to 400°F.
3. Toss the bread cubes into the air fryer and air-fry for 7 minutes, shaking the basket once or twice while they cook.
4. Serve warm or store in an airtight container.

Eggplant Parmesan Subs

Servings: 2 | Cooking Time: 13 Minutes

Ingredients:

- 4 Peeled eggplant slices
- Olive oil spray
- 2 tablespoons plus 2 teaspoons Jarred pizza sauce, any variety except creamy
- ¼ cup (about ⅔ ounce) Finely grated Parmesan cheese
- 2 Small, long soft rolls, such as hero, hoagie, or Italian sub rolls (gluten-free, if a concern), split open lengthwise

Directions:

1. Preheat the air fryer to 350°F .
2. When the machine is at temperature, coat both sides of the eggplant slices with olive oil spray. Set them in the basket in one layer and air-fry undisturbed for 10 minutes, until lightly browned and softened.
3. Increase the machine's temperature to 375°F. Top each eggplant slice with 2 teaspoons pizza sauce, then 1 tablespoon cheese. Air-fry undisturbed for 2 minutes, or until the cheese has melted.
4. Use a nonstick-safe spatula, and perhaps a flatware fork for balance, to transfer the eggplant slices cheese side up to a cutting board. Set the roll(s) cut side down in the basket in one layer and air-fry undisturbed for 1 minute, to toast the rolls a bit and warm them up. Set 2 eggplant slices in each warm roll.

Fry Bread

Servings: 4 | Cooking Time: 5 Minutes

Ingredients:

- 1 cup flour
- 2 teaspoons baking powder
- ¼ teaspoon salt
- ¼ cup lukewarm milk
- 1 teaspoon oil
- 2–3 tablespoons water
- oil for misting or cooking spray

Directions:

1. Stir together flour, baking powder, and salt. Gently mix in the milk and oil. Stir in 1 tablespoon water. If needed, add more water 1 tablespoon at a time until stiff dough forms. Dough shouldn't be sticky, so use only as much as you need.
2. Divide dough into 4 portions and shape into balls. Cover with a towel and let rest for 10minutes.
3. Preheat air fryer to 390°F.
4. Shape dough as desired:
5. a. Pat into 3-inch circles. This will make a thicker bread to eat plain or with a sprinkle of cinnamon or honey butter. You can cook all 4 at once.
6. b. Pat thinner into rectangles about 3 x 6 inches. This will create a thinner bread to serve as a base for dishes such as Indian tacos. The circular shape is more traditional, but rectangles allow you to cook 2 at a time in your air fryer basket.
7. Spray both sides of dough pieces with oil or cooking spray.
8. Place the 4 circles or 2 of the dough rectangles in the air fryer basket and cook at 390°F for 3minutes. Spray tops, turn, spray other side, and cook for 2 more minutes. If necessary, repeat to cook remaining bread.
9. Serve piping hot as is or allow to cool slightly and add toppings to create your own Native American tacos.

Tuna And Arugula Salad

Servings: 4 | Cooking Time: 15 Minutes

Ingredients:

- ½ pound smoked tuna, flaked
- 1 cup arugula
- 2 spring onions, chopped
- 1 tablespoon olive oil
- A pinch of salt and black pepper

Directions:

1. In a bowl, all the ingredients except the oil and the arugula and whisk. Preheat the Air Fryer over 360°F, add the oil and grease it. Pour the tuna mix, stir well, and cook for 15 minutes. In a salad bowl, combine the arugula with the tuna mix, toss and serve for breakfast.

Bacon Eggs

Servings: 2 | Cooking Time: 5 Minutes

Ingredients:
- 2 eggs, hard-boiled, peeled
- 4 bacon slices
- ½ teaspoon avocado oil
- 1 teaspoon mustard

Directions:

1. Preheat the air fryer to 400°F. Then sprinkle the air fryer basket with avocado oil and place the bacon slices inside. Flatten them in one layer and cook for 2 minutes from each side. After this, cool the bacon to the room temperature. Wrap every egg into 2 bacon slices. Secure the eggs with toothpicks and place them in the air fryer. Cook the wrapped eggs for 1 minute at 400°F.

Thai Turkey Sausage Patties

Servings:4 | Cooking Time: 30 Minutes

Ingredients:
- 12 oz turkey sausage
- 1 tsp onion powder
- 1 tsp dried coriander
- ¼ tsp Thai curry paste
- ¼ tsp red pepper flakes
- Salt and pepper to taste

Directions:

1. Preheat air fryer to 350°F. Place the sausage, onion, coriander, curry paste, red flakes, salt, and black pepper in a large bowl and mix well. Form into eight patties. Arrange the patties on the greased frying basket and Air Fry for 10 minutes, flipping once halfway through. Once the patties are cooked, transfer to a plate and serve hot.

Chapter 4 Poultry Recipes

Chapter 4 Poultry Recipes

Easy & Crispy Chicken Wings

Servings: 8 | Cooking Time: 20 Minutes

Ingredients:

- 1 1/2 lbs chicken wings
- 2 tbsp olive oil
- Pepper
- Salt

Directions:

1. Toss chicken wings with oil and place in the air fryer basket.
2. Cook chicken wings at 370°F for 15 minutes.
3. Shake basket and cook at 400 F for 5 minutes more.
4. Season chicken wings with pepper and salt.
5. Serve and enjoy.

Turkey-hummus Wraps

Servings: 4 | Cooking Time: 7 Minutes Per Batch

Ingredients:

- 4 large whole wheat wraps
- ½ cup hummus
- 16 thin slices deli turkey
- 8 slices provolone cheese
- 1 cup fresh baby spinach (or more to taste)

Directions:

1. To assemble, place 2 tablespoons of hummus on each wrap and spread to within about a half inch from edges. Top with 4 slices of turkey and 2 slices of provolone. Finish with ¼ cup of baby spinach—or pile on as much as you like.
2. Roll up each wrap. You don't need to fold or seal the ends.
3. Place 2 wraps in air fryer basket, seam side down.
4. Cook at 360°F for 4minutes to warm filling and melt cheese. If you like, you can continue cooking for 3 more minutes, until the wrap is slightly crispy.
5. Repeat step 4 to cook remaining wraps.

Ginger Turmeric Chicken Thighs

Servings:4 | Cooking Time: 25 Minutes

Ingredients:

- 4 boneless, skin-on chicken thighs
- 2 tablespoons coconut oil, melted
- ½ teaspoon ground turmeric
- ½ teaspoon salt
- ½ teaspoon garlic powder
- ½ teaspoon ground ginger
- ¼ teaspoon ground black pepper

Directions:

1. Place chicken thighs in a large bowl and drizzle with coconut oil. Sprinkle with remaining ingredients and toss to coat both sides of thighs.
2. Place thighs skin side up into ungreased air fryer basket. Adjust the temperature to 400°F and set the timer for 25 minutes. After 10 minutes, turn thighs. When 5 minutes remain, flip thighs once more. Chicken will be done when skin is golden brown and the internal temperature is at least 165°F. Serve warm.

Yummy Shredded Chicken

Servings: 2 | Cooking Time: 15 Minutes

Ingredients:

- 2 large chicken breasts
- ¼ tsp Pepper
- 1 tsp garlic puree
- 1 tsp mustard
- Salt

Directions:

1. Add all ingredients to the bowl and toss well.
2. Transfer chicken into the air fryer basket and cook at 360°F for 15 minutes.
3. Remove chicken from air fryer and shred using a fork.
4. Serve and enjoy.

Za'atar Chicken Drumsticks

Servings: 4 | Cooking Time: 45 Minutes

Ingredients:

- 2 tbsp butter, melted
- 8 chicken drumsticks
- 1 ½ tbsp Za'atar seasoning
- Salt and pepper to taste
- 1 lemon, zested
- 2 tbsp parsley, chopped

Directions:

1. Preheat air fryer to 390°F. Mix the Za'atar seasoning, lemon zest, parsley, salt, and pepper in a bowl. Add the chicken drumsticks and toss to coat. Place them in the air fryer and brush them with butter. Air Fry for 18-20 minutes, flipping once until crispy. Serve and enjoy!

Garlic Parmesan Drumsticks

Servings:4 | Cooking Time: 25 Minutes

Ingredients:
- 8 chicken drumsticks
- ½ teaspoon salt
- ⅛ teaspoon ground black pepper
- ½ teaspoon garlic powder
- 2 tablespoons salted butter, melted
- ½ cup grated Parmesan cheese
- 1 tablespoon dried parsley

Directions:

1. Sprinkle drumsticks with salt, pepper, and garlic powder. Place drumsticks into ungreased air fryer basket.
2. Adjust the temperature to 400°F and set the timer for 25 minutes, turning drumsticks halfway through cooking. Drumsticks will be golden and have an internal temperature of at least 165°F when done.
3. Transfer drumsticks to a large serving dish. Pour butter over drumsticks, and sprinkle with Parmesan and parsley. Serve warm.

Chicken–cream Cheese Taquitos

Servings:4 | Cooking Time: 8 Minutes

Ingredients:
- 1 ½ cups shredded cooked chicken
- 4 ounces full-fat cream cheese, softened
- 1 cup shredded sharp Cheddar cheese
- 12 white corn tortillas

Directions:

1. Preheat the air fryer to 350°F.
2. In a large bowl, mix chicken, cream cheese, and Cheddar.
3. Place 3 tablespoons chicken mixture onto each tortilla and roll. Spritz each roll with cooking spray.
4. Place seam side down in the air fryer basket and cook 8 minutes, turning halfway through cooking time, until crispy and brown. Serve warm.

Cheesy Chicken Nuggets

Servings:4 | Cooking Time: 15 Minutes

Ingredients:
- 1 pound ground chicken thighs
- ½ cup shredded mozzarella cheese
- 1 large egg, whisked
- ½ teaspoon salt
- ¼ teaspoon dried oregano
- ¼ teaspoon garlic powder

Directions:

1. In a large bowl, combine all ingredients. Form mixture into twenty nugget shapes, about 2 tablespoons each.
2. Place nuggets into ungreased air fryer basket, working in batches if needed. Adjust the temperature to 375°F and set the timer for 15 minutes, turning nuggets halfway through cooking. Let cool 5 minutes before serving.

Servings:4 | Cooking Time: 12 Minutes

Ingredients:

- 1 pound boneless, skinless chicken tenders
- 2 teaspoons paprika
- 1 teaspoon garlic powder
- 1 teaspoon salt
- ½ teaspoon cayenne pepper
- ½ teaspoon dried thyme
- ½ teaspoon ground black pepper
- Cooking spray

Directions:

1. Preheat the air fryer to 400°F.
2. Place chicken tenders into a large bowl.
3. In a small bowl, mix paprika, garlic powder, salt, cayenne, thyme, and black pepper. Add spice mixture to chicken and toss to coat. Spritz chicken with cooking spray.
4. Place chicken in the air fryer basket and cook 12 minutes, turning halfway through cooking time, until chicken is brown at the edges and internal temperature reaches at least 165°F. Serve warm.

Buttermilk-fried Chicken Thighs

Servings:4 | Cooking Time: 1 Hour

Ingredients:

- 1 cup buttermilk
- 2 tablespoons seasoned salt, divided
- 1 pound bone-in, skin-on chicken thighs
- 1 cup all-purpose flour
- ¼ cup cornstarch

Directions:

1. In a large bowl, combine buttermilk and 1 tablespoon seasoned salt. Add chicken. Cover and let marinate in refrigerator 30 minutes.
2. Preheat the air fryer to 375°F.
3. In a separate bowl, mix flour, cornstarch, and remaining seasoned salt. Dredge chicken thighs, one at a time, in flour mixture, covering completely.
4. Spray chicken generously with cooking spray, being sure that no dry spots remain. Place chicken in the air fryer basket and cook 30 minutes, turning halfway through cooking time and spraying any dry spots, until chicken is dark golden brown and crispy and internal temperature reaches at least 165°F.
5. Serve warm.

Spinach 'n Bacon Egg Cups

Servings:4 | Cooking Time: 10 Minutes

Ingredients:
- ¼ cup spinach, chopped finely
- 1 bacon strip, fried and crumbled
- 3 tablespoons butter
- 4 eggs, beaten
- Salt and pepper to taste

Directions:
1. Preheat the air fryer for 5 minutes.
2. In a mixing bowl, combine the eggs, butter, and spinach. Season with salt and pepper to taste.
3. Grease a ramekin with cooking spray and pour the egg mixture inside.
4. Sprinkle with bacon bits.
5. Place the ramekin in the air fryer.
6. Cook for 10 minutes at 350°F.

Creamy Onion Chicken

Servings:4 | Cooking Time: 20 Minutes

Ingredients:
- 1 ½ cup onion soup mix
- 1 cup mushroom soup
- ½ cup cream

Directions:

1. Preheat Fryer to 400°F. Add mushrooms, onion mix and cream in a frying pan. Heat on low heat for 1 minute. Pour the warm mixture over chicken slices and allow to sit for 25 minutes. Place the marinated chicken in the air fryer cooking basket and cook for 15 minutes. Serve with the remaining cream.

Lemon Pepper Chicken Wings

Servings: 4 | Cooking Time: 16 Minutes

Ingredients:

- 1 lb chicken wings
- 1 tsp lemon pepper
- 1 tbsp olive oil
- 1 tsp salt

Directions:

1. Add chicken wings into the large mixing bowl.
2. Add remaining ingredients over chicken and toss well to coat.
3. Place chicken wings in the air fryer basket.
4. Cook chicken wings for 8 minutes at 400°F.
5. Turn chicken wings to another side and cook for 8 minutes more.
6. Serve and enjoy.

Chicken Wrapped In Bacon

Servings: 6 | Cooking Time: 25 Minutes

Ingredients:

- 6 rashers unsmoked back bacon
- 1 small chicken breast
- 1 tbsp. garlic soft cheese

Directions:

1. Cut the chicken breast into six bite-sized pieces.
2. Spread the soft cheese across one side of each slice of bacon.
3. Put the chicken on top of the cheese and wrap the bacon around it, holding it in place with a toothpick.
4. Transfer the wrapped chicken pieces to the Air Fryer and cook for 15 minutes at 350°F.

Chicken Wings

Servings: 4 | Cooking Time: 55 Minutes

Ingredients:

- 3 lb. bone-in chicken wings
- ¾ cup flour
- 1 tbsp. old bay seasoning
- 4 tbsp. butter
- Couple fresh lemons

Directions:

1. In a bowl, combine the all-purpose flour and Old Bay seasoning.
2. Toss the chicken wings with the mixture to coat each one well.
3. Pre-heat the Air Fryer to 375°F.
4. Give the wings a shake to shed any excess flour and place each one in the Air Fryer. You may have to do this in multiple batches, so as to not overlap any.
5. Cook for 30 – 40 minutes, shaking the basket frequently, until the wings are cooked through and crispy.
6. In the meantime, melt the butter in a frying pan over a low heat. Squeeze one or two lemons and add the juice to the pan. Mix well.
7. Serve the wings topped with the sauce.

Perfect Grill Chicken Breast

Servings: 2 | Cooking Time: 12 Minutes

Ingredients:

- 2 chicken breast, skinless and boneless
- 2 tsp olive oil
- Pepper
- Salt

Directions:

1. Remove air fryer basket and replace it with air fryer grill pan.
2. Place chicken breast to the grill pan. Season chicken with pepper and salt. Drizzle with oil.
3. Cook chicken for 375°F for 12 minutes.
4. Serve and enjoy.

Crunchy Chicken Strips

Servings: 4 | Cooking Time: 40 Minutes

Ingredients:

- 1 chicken breast, sliced into strips
- 1 tbsp grated Parmesan cheese
- 1 cup breadcrumbs
- 1 tbsp chicken seasoning
- 2 eggs, beaten
- Salt and pepper to taste

Directions:

1. Preheat air fryer to 350°F. Mix the breadcrumbs, Parmesan cheese, chicken seasoning, salt, and pepper in a mixing bowl. Coat the chicken with the crumb mixture, then dip in the beaten eggs. Finally, coat again with the dry ingredients. Arrange the coated chicken pieces on the greased frying basket and Air Fry for 15 minutes. Turn over halfway through cooking and cook for another 15 minutes. Serve immediately.

Bacon Chicken Mix

Servings: 2 | Cooking Time: 25 Minutes

Ingredients:

- 2 chicken legs
- 4 oz bacon, sliced
- ½ teaspoon salt
- ½ teaspoon ground black pepper
- 1 teaspoon sesame oil

Directions:

1. Sprinkle the chicken legs with salt and ground black pepper and wrap in the sliced bacon. After this, preheat the air fryer to 385°F. Put the chicken legs in the air fryer and sprinkle with sesame oil. Cook the bacon chicken legs for 25 minutes.

Hot Chicken Skin

Servings: 4 | Cooking Time: 30 Minutes

Ingredients:
- ½ teaspoon chili paste
- 8 oz chicken skin
- 1 teaspoon sesame oil
- ½ teaspoon chili powder
- ½ teaspoon salt

Directions:

1. In the shallow bowl mix up chili paste, sesame oil, chili powder, and salt. Then brush the chicken skin with chili mixture well and leave for 10 minutes to marinate. Meanwhile, preheat the air fryer to 365°F. Put the marinated chicken skin in the air fryer and cook it for 20 minutes. When the time is finished, flip the chicken skin on another side and cook it for 10 minutes more or until the chicken skin is crunchy.

Family Chicken Fingers

Servings: 4 | Cooking Time: 30 Minutes

Ingredients:
- 1 lb chicken breast fingers
- 1 tbsp chicken seasoning
- ½ tsp mustard powder
- Salt and pepper to taste
- 2 eggs
- 1 cup bread crumbs

Directions:

1. Preheat air fryer to 400°F. Add the chicken fingers to a large bowl along with chicken seasoning, mustard, salt, and pepper; mix well. Set up two small bowls. In one bowl, beat the eggs. In the second bowl, add the bread crumbs. Dip the chicken in the egg, then dredge in breadcrumbs. Place the nuggets in the air fryer. Lightly spray with cooking oil, then Air Fry for 8 minutes, shaking the basket once until crispy and cooked through. Serve warm.

Air Fried Chicken Tenderloin

Servings:8 | Cooking Time: 15 Minutes

Ingredients:
- ½ cup almond flour
- 1 egg, beaten
- 2 tablespoons coconut oil
- 8 chicken tenderloins
- Salt and pepper to taste

Directions:
1. Preheat the air fryer for 5 minutes.
2. Season the chicken tenderloin with salt and pepper to taste.
3. Soak in beaten eggs then dredge in almond flour.
4. Place in the air fryer and brush with coconut oil.
5. Cook for 15 minutes at 375°F.
6. Halfway through the cooking time, give the fryer basket a shake to cook evenly.

Chicken & Pepperoni Pizza

Servings: 6 | Cooking Time: 20 Minutes

Ingredients:
- 2 cups cooked chicken, cubed
- 20 slices pepperoni
- 1 cup sugar-free pizza sauce
- 1 cup mozzarella cheese, shredded
- ¼ cup parmesan cheese, grated

Directions:
1. Place the chicken into the base of a four-cup baking dish and add the pepperoni and pizza sauce on top. Mix well so as to completely coat the meat with the sauce.
2. Add the parmesan and mozzarella on top of the chicken, then place the baking dish into your fryer.
3. Cook for 15 minutes at 375°F.
4. When everything is bubbling and melted, remove from the fryer. Serve hot.

Chapter 5 Beef , Pork & Lamb Recipes

Chapter 5 Beef , Pork & Lamb Recipes

Parmesan-crusted Pork Chops

Servings:4 | Cooking Time: 12 Minutes

Ingredients:

- 1 large egg
- ½ cup grated Parmesan cheese
- 4 boneless pork chops
- ½ teaspoon salt
- ¼ teaspoon ground black pepper

Directions:

1. Whisk egg in a medium bowl and place Parmesan in a separate medium bowl.
2. Sprinkle pork chops on both sides with salt and pepper. Dip each pork chop into egg, then press both sides into Parmesan.
3. Place pork chops into ungreased air fryer basket. Adjust the temperature to 400°F and set the timer for 12 minutes, turning chops halfway through cooking. Pork chops will be golden and have an internal temperature of at least 145°F when done. Serve warm.

Sweet And Spicy Spare Ribs

Servings:6 | Cooking Time: 30 Minutes

Ingredients:

- ¼ cup granular brown erythritol
- 2 teaspoons paprika
- 2 teaspoons chili powder
- 1 teaspoon garlic powder
- ½ teaspoon cayenne pepper
- 2 teaspoons salt
- 1 teaspoon ground black pepper
- 1 rack pork spare ribs

Directions:

1. In a small bowl, mix erythritol, paprika, chili powder, garlic powder, cayenne pepper, salt, and black pepper. Rub spice mix over ribs on both sides. Place ribs on ungreased aluminum foil sheet and wrap to cover.
2. Place ribs into ungreased air fryer basket. Adjust the temperature to 400°F and set the timer for 25 minutes.
3. When timer beeps, remove ribs from foil, then place back into air fryer basket to cook an additional 5 minutes, turning halfway through cooking. Ribs will be browned and have an internal temperature of at least 180°F when done. Serve warm.

Mozzarella-stuffed Meatloaf

Servings:6 | Cooking Time: 30 Minutes

Ingredients:
- 1 pound 80/20 ground beef
- ½ medium green bell pepper, seeded and chopped
- ¼ medium yellow onion, peeled and chopped
- ½ teaspoon salt
- ¼ teaspoon ground black pepper
- 2 ounces mozzarella cheese, sliced into ¼"-thick slices
- ¼ cup low-carb ketchup

Directions:

1. In a large bowl, combine ground beef, bell pepper, onion, salt, and black pepper. Cut a piece of parchment to fit air fryer basket. Place half beef mixture on ungreased parchment and form a 9" × 4" loaf, about ½" thick.
2. Center mozzarella slices on beef loaf, leaving at least ¼" around each edge.
3. Press remaining beef into a second 9" × 4" loaf and place on top of mozzarella, pressing edges of loaves together to seal.
4. Place parchment with meatloaf into air fryer basket. Adjust the temperature to 350°F and set the timer for 30 minutes, carefully turning loaf and brushing top with ketchup halfway through cooking. Loaf will be browned and have an internal temperature of at least 180°F when done. Slice and serve warm.

Hot Dogs

Servings:8 | Cooking Time: 7 Minutes

Ingredients:
- 8 beef hot dogs
- 8 hot dog buns

Directions:

1. Preheat the air fryer to 400°F.
2. Place hot dogs in the air fryer basket and cook 7 minutes. Place each hot dog in a bun. Serve warm.

Cheeseburgers

Servings:4 | Cooking Time: 10 Hours

Ingredients:
- 1 pound 70/30 ground beef
- ½ teaspoon salt
- ¼ teaspoon ground black pepper
- 4 slices American cheese
- 4 hamburger buns

Directions:

1. Preheat the air fryer to 360°F.
2. Separate beef into four equal portions and form into patties.
3. Sprinkle both sides of patties with salt and pepper. Place in the air fryer basket and cook 10 minutes, turning halfway through cooking time, until internal temperature reaches at least 160°F.
4. For each burger, place a slice of cheese on a patty and place on a hamburger bun. Serve warm.

Tonkatsu

Servings: 3 | Cooking Time: 10 Minutes

Ingredients:

- ½ cup All-purpose flour or tapioca flour
- 1 Large egg white(s), well beaten
- ¾ cup Plain panko bread crumbs (gluten-free, if a concern)
- 3 4-ounce center-cut boneless pork loin chops (about ½ inch thick)
- Vegetable oil spray

Directions:

1. Preheat the air fryer to 375°F .
2. Set up and fill three shallow soup plates or small pie plates on your counter: one for the flour, one for the beaten egg white(s), and one for the bread crumbs.
3. Set a chop in the flour and roll it to coat all sides, even the ends. Gently shake off any excess flour and set it in the egg white(s). Gently roll and turn it to coat all sides. Let any excess egg white slip back into the rest, then set the chop in the bread crumbs. Turn it several times, pressing gently to get an even coating on all sides and the ends. Generously coat the breaded chop with vegetable oil spray, then set it aside so you can dredge, coat, and spray the remaining chop(s).
4. Set the chops in the basket with as much air space between them as possible. Air-fry undisturbed for 10 minutes, or until golden brown and crisp.
5. Use kitchen tongs to transfer the chops to a wire rack and cool for a couple of minutes before serving.

Barbecue Country-style Pork Ribs

Servings: 3 | Cooking Time: 30 Minutes

Ingredients:

- 3 8-ounce boneless country-style pork ribs
- 1½ teaspoons Mild smoked paprika
- 1½ teaspoons Light brown sugar
- ¾ teaspoon Onion powder
- ¾ teaspoon Ground black pepper
- ¼ teaspoon Table salt
- Vegetable oil spray

Directions:

1. Preheat the air fryer to 350°F . Set the ribs in a bowl on the counter as the machine heats.
2. Mix the smoked paprika, brown sugar, onion powder, pepper, and salt in a small bowl until well combined. Rub this mixture over all the surfaces of the country-style ribs. Generously coat the country-style ribs with vegetable oil spray.
3. Set the ribs in the basket with as much air space between them as possible. Air-fry undisturbed for 30 minutes, or until browned and sizzling and an instant-read meat thermometer inserted into one rib registers at least 145°F.
4. Use kitchen tongs to transfer the country-style ribs to a wire rack. Cool for 5 minutes before serving.

Lamb Chops

Servings: 2 | Cooking Time: 20 Minutes

Ingredients:
- 2 teaspoons oil
- ½ teaspoon ground rosemary
- ½ teaspoon lemon juice
- 1 pound lamb chops, approximately 1-inch thick
- salt and pepper
- cooking spray

Directions:

1. Mix the oil, rosemary, and lemon juice together and rub into all sides of the lamb chops. Season to taste with salt and pepper.
2. For best flavor, cover lamb chops and allow them to rest in the fridge for 20 minutes.
3. Spray air fryer basket with nonstick spray and place lamb chops in it.
4. Cook at 360°F for approximately 20minutes. This will cook chops to medium. The meat will be juicy but have no remaining pink. Cook for a minute or two longer for well done chops. For rare chops, stop cooking after about 12minutes and check for doneness.

Rib Eye Steak Seasoned With Italian Herb

Servings:4 | Cooking Time: 45 Minutes

Ingredients:
- 1 packet Italian herb mix
- 1 tablespoon olive oil
- 2 pounds bone-in rib eye steak
- Salt and pepper to taste

Directions:

1. Preheat the air fryer to 390°F.
2. Place the grill pan accessory in the air fryer.
3. Season the steak with salt, pepper, Italian herb mix, and olive oil. Cover top with foil.
4. Grill for 45 minutes and flip the steak halfway through the cooking time.

Pork Spare Ribs

Servings:4 | Cooking Time: 30 Minutes

Ingredients:

- 1 rack pork spare ribs
- 1 teaspoon ground cumin
- 2 teaspoons salt
- 1 teaspoon ground black pepper
- 1 teaspoon garlic powder
- ½ teaspoon dry ground mustard
- ½ cup low-carb barbecue sauce

Directions:

1. Place ribs on ungreased aluminum foil sheet. Carefully use a knife to remove membrane and sprinkle meat evenly on both sides with cumin, salt, pepper, garlic powder, and ground mustard.
2. Cut rack into portions that will fit in your air fryer, and wrap each portion in one layer of aluminum foil, working in batches if needed.
3. Place ribs into ungreased air fryer basket. Adjust the temperature to 400°F and set the timer for 25 minutes.
4. When the timer beeps, carefully remove ribs from foil and brush with barbecue sauce. Return to air fryer and cook at 400°F for an additional 5 minutes to brown. Ribs will be done when no pink remains and internal temperature is at least 180°F. Serve warm.

Simple Beef

Servings: 1 | Cooking Time: 25 Minutes

Ingredients:

- 1 thin beef schnitzel
- 1 egg, beaten
- ½ cup friendly bread crumbs
- 2 tbsp. olive oil
- Pepper and salt to taste

Directions:

1. Pre-heat the Air Fryer to 350°F.
2. In a shallow dish, combine the bread crumbs, oil, pepper, and salt.
3. In a second shallow dish, place the beaten egg.
4. Dredge the schnitzel in the egg before rolling it in the bread crumbs.
5. Put the coated schnitzel in the fryer basket and air fry for 12 minutes.

Bacon And Cheese–stuffed Pork Chops

Servings:4 | Cooking Time: 12 Minutes

Ingredients:

- ½ ounce plain pork rinds, finely crushed
- ½ cup shredded sharp Cheddar cheese
- 4 slices cooked sugar-free bacon, crumbled
- 4 boneless pork chops
- ½ teaspoon salt
- ¼ teaspoon ground black pepper

Directions:

1. In a small bowl, mix pork rinds, Cheddar, and bacon.
2. Make a 3" slit in the side of each pork chop and stuff with ¼ pork rind mixture. Sprinkle each side of pork chops with salt and pepper.
3. Place pork chops into ungreased air fryer basket, stuffed side up. Adjust the temperature to 400°F and set the timer for 12 minutes. Pork chops will be browned and have an internal temperature of at least 145°F when done. Serve warm.

Cheddar Bacon Ranch Pinwheels

Servings:5 | Cooking Time: 12 Minutes Per Batch

Ingredients:

- 4 ounces full-fat cream cheese, softened
- 1 tablespoon dry ranch seasoning
- ½ cup shredded Cheddar cheese
- 1 sheet frozen puff pastry dough, thawed
- 6 slices bacon, cooked and crumbled

Directions:

1. Preheat the air fryer to 320°F. Cut parchment paper to fit the air fryer basket.
2. In a medium bowl, mix cream cheese, ranch seasoning, and Cheddar. Unfold puff pastry and gently spread cheese mixture over pastry.
3. Sprinkle crumbled bacon on top. Starting from a long side, roll dough into a log, pressing in the edges to seal.
4. Cut log into ten pieces, then place on parchment in the air fryer basket, working in batches as necessary.
5. Cook 12 minutes, turning each piece after 7 minutes. Let cool 5 minutes before serving.

Bacon With Shallot And Greens

Servings: 2 | Cooking Time: 10 Minutes

Ingredients:

- 7 ounces mixed greens
- 8 thick slices pork bacon
- 2 shallots, peeled and diced
- Nonstick cooking spray

Directions:

1. Begin by preheating the air fryer to 345°F.
2. Now, add the shallot and bacon to the Air Fryer cooking basket; set the timer for 2 minutes. Spritz with a nonstick cooking spray.
3. After that, pause the Air Fryer; throw in the mixed greens; give it a good stir and cook an additional 5 minutes. Serve warm.

Wasabi-coated Pork Loin Chops

Servings: 3 | Cooking Time: 14 Minutes

Ingredients:

- 1½ cups Wasabi peas
- ¼ cup Plain panko bread crumbs
- 1 Large egg white(s)
- 2 tablespoons Water
- 3 5- to 6-ounce boneless center-cut pork loin chops (about ½ inch thick)

Directions:

1. Preheat the air fryer to 375°F.
2. Put the wasabi peas in a food processor. Cover and process until finely ground, about like panko bread crumbs. Add the bread crumbs and pulse a few times to blend.
3. Set up and fill two shallow soup plates or small pie plates on your counter: one for the egg white(s), whisked with the water until uniform; and one for the wasabi pea mixture.
4. Dip a pork chop in the egg white mixture, coating the chop on both sides as well as around the edge. Allow any excess egg white mixture to slip back into the rest, then set the chop in the wasabi pea mixture. Press gently and turn it several times to coat evenly on both sides and around the edge. Set aside, then dip and coat the remaining chop(s).
5. Set the chops in the basket with as much air space between them as possible. Air-fry, turning once at the 6-minute mark, for 12 minutes, or until the chops are crisp and browned and an instant-read meat thermometer inserted into the center of a chop registers 145°F. If the machine is at 360°F, you may need to add 2 minutes to the cooking time.
6. Use kitchen tongs to transfer the chops to a wire rack. Cool for a couple of minutes before serving.

Mustard Pork

Servings: 4 | Cooking Time: 30 Minutes

Ingredients:
- 1 pound pork tenderloin, trimmed
- A pinch of salt and black pepper
- 2 tablespoons olive oil
- 3 tablespoons mustard
- 2 tablespoons balsamic vinegar

Directions:

1. In a bowl, mix the pork tenderloin with the rest of the ingredients and rub well. Put the roast in your air fryer's basket and cook at 380°F for 30 minutes. Slice the roast, divide between plates and serve.

Empanadas

Servings:4 | Cooking Time: 28 Minutes

Ingredients:
- 1 pound 80/20 ground beef
- ¼ cup taco seasoning
- ⅓ cup salsa
- 2 refrigerated piecrusts
- 1 cup shredded Colby-jack cheese

Directions:

1. In a medium skillet over medium heat, brown beef about 10 minutes until cooked through. Drain fat, then add taco seasoning and salsa to the pan. Bring to a boil, then cook 30 seconds. Reduce heat and simmer 5 minutes. Remove from heat.
2. Preheat the air fryer to 370°F.
3. Cut three 5" circles from each piecrust, forming six total. Reroll scraps out to ½" thickness. Cut out two more 5" circles to make eight circles total.
4. For each empanada, place ¼ cup meat mixture onto the lower half of a pastry circle and top with 2 tablespoons cheese. Dab a little water along the edge of pastry and fold circle in half to fully cover meat and cheese, pressing the edges together. Use a fork to gently seal the edges. Repeat with remaining pastry, meat, and cheese.
5. Spritz empanadas with cooking spray. Place in the air fryer basket and cook 12 minutes, turning halfway through cooking time, until crust is golden. Serve warm.

Chicken Fried Steak

Servings: 4 | Cooking Time: 15 Minutes

Ingredients:

- 2 eggs
- ½ cup buttermilk
- 1½ cups flour
- ¾ teaspoon salt
- ½ teaspoon pepper
- 1 pound beef cube steaks
- salt and pepper
- oil for misting or cooking spray

Directions:

1. Beat together eggs and buttermilk in a shallow dish.
2. In another shallow dish, stir together the flour, ½ teaspoon salt, and ¼ teaspoon pepper.
3. Season cube steaks with remaining salt and pepper to taste. Dip in flour, buttermilk egg wash, and then flour again.
4. Spray both sides of steaks with oil or cooking spray.
5. Cooking in 2 batches, place steaks in air fryer basket in single layer. Cook at 360°F for 10minutes. Spray tops of steaks with oil and cook 5minutes or until meat is well done.
6. Repeat to cook remaining steaks.

Sesame Lamb Chops

Servings: 6 | Cooking Time: 11 Minutes

Ingredients:

- 6 lamb chops
- 1 tablespoon sesame oil
- 1 tablespoon za'atar seasonings

Directions:

1. Rub the lamb chops with za'atar seasonings and sprinkle with sesame oil. Preheat the air fryer to 400°F. Then arrange the lamb chops in the air fryer in one layer and cook them for 5 minutes. Then flip the pork chops on another side and cook them for 6 minutes more.

Crispy Five-spice Pork Belly

Servings: 6 | Cooking Time: 60-75 Minutes

Ingredients:

- 1½ pounds Pork belly with skin
- 3 tablespoons Shaoxing (Chinese cooking rice wine), dry sherry, or white grape juice
- 1½ teaspoons Granulated white sugar
- ¾ teaspoon Five-spice powder
- 1¼ cups Coarse sea salt or kosher salt

Directions:

1. Preheat the air fryer to 350°F .
2. Set the pork belly skin side up on a cutting board. Use a meat fork to make dozens and dozens of tiny holes all across the surface of the skin. You can hardly make too many holes. These will allow the skin to bubble up and keep it from becoming hard as it roasts.
3. Turn the pork belly over so that one of its longer sides faces you. Make four evenly spaced vertical slits in the meat. The slits should go about halfway into the meat toward the fat.
4. Mix the Shaoxing or its substitute, sugar, and five-spice powder in a small bowl until the sugar dissolves. Massage this mixture across the meat and into the cuts.
5. Turn the pork belly over again. Blot dry any moisture on the skin. Make a double-thickness aluminum foil tray by setting two 10-inch-long pieces of foil on top of another. Set the pork belly skin side up in the center of this tray. Fold the sides of the tray up toward the pork, crimping the foil as you work to make a high-sided case all around the pork belly. Seal the foil to the meat on all sides so that only the skin is exposed.
6. Pour the salt onto the skin and pat it down and in place to create a crust. Pick up the foil tray with the pork in it and set it in the basket.
7. Air-fry undisturbed for 35 minutes for a small batch, 45 minutes for a medium batch, or 50 minutes for a large batch.
8. Remove the foil tray with the pork belly still in it. Warning: The foil tray is full of scalding-hot fat. Discard the fat in the tray, as well as the tray itself. Transfer the pork belly to a cutting board.
9. Raise the air fryer temperature to 375°F. Brush the salt crust off the pork, removing any visible salt from the sides of the meat, too.
10. When the machine is at temperature, return the pork belly skin side up to the basket. Air-fry undisturbed for 25 minutes, or until crisp and very well browned. If the machine is at 390°F, you may be able to shave 5 minutes off the cooking time so that the skin doesn't blacken.
11. Use a nonstick-safe spatula, and perhaps a silicone baking mitt, to transfer the pork belly to a wire rack. Cool for 10 minutes before serving.

Rib Eye Steak

Servings:4 | Cooking Time: 15 Minutes

Ingredients:

- 4 rib eye steaks
- 1 teaspoon salt
- ½ teaspoon ground black pepper
- 2 tablespoons salted butter

Directions:

1. Preheat the air fryer to 400°F.
2. Sprinkle steaks with salt and pepper and place in the air fryer basket.
3. Cook 15 minutes, turning halfway through cooking time, until edges are firm, and the internal temperature reaches at least 160°F for well-done.
4. Top each steak with ½ tablespoon butter immediately after removing from the air fryer. Let rest 5 minutes before cutting. Serve warm.

Chapter 6 Fish And Seafood Recipes

Chapter 6 Fish And Seafood Recipes

Cajun Lobster Tails

Servings:4 | Cooking Time: 10 Minutes

Ingredients:

- 4 lobster tails
- 2 tablespoons salted butter, melted
- 2 teaspoons lemon juice
- 1 tablespoon Cajun seasoning

Directions:

1. Preheat the air fryer to 400°F.
2. Carefully cut open lobster tails with kitchen scissors and pull back the shell a little to expose the meat. Drizzle butter and lemon juice over each tail, then sprinkle with Cajun seasoning.
3. Place tails in the air fryer basket and cook 10 minutes until lobster shells are bright red and internal temperature reaches at least 145°F. Serve warm.

Simple Sesame Squid On The Grill

Servings:3 | Cooking Time: 10 Minutes

Ingredients:

- 1 ½ pounds squid, cleaned
- 2 tablespoon toasted sesame oil
- Salt and pepper to taste

Directions:

1. Preheat the air fryer at 390°F.
2. Place the grill pan accessory in the air fryer.
3. Season the squid with sesame oil, salt and pepper.
4. Grill the squid for 10 minutes.

Fish Sticks For Kids

Servings: 8 | Cooking Time: 6 Minutes

Ingredients:

- 8 ounces fish fillets (pollock or cod)
- salt (optional)
- ½ cup plain breadcrumbs
- oil for misting or cooking spray

Directions:

1. Cut fish fillets into "fingers" about ½ x 3 inches. Sprinkle with salt to taste, if desired.
2. Roll fish in breadcrumbs. Spray all sides with oil or cooking spray.
3. Place in air fryer basket in single layer and cook at 390°F for 6 minutes, until golden brown and crispy.

Sea Scallops

Servings: 4 | Cooking Time: 8 Minutes

Ingredients:

- 1½ pounds sea scallops
- salt and pepper
- 2 eggs
- ½ cup flour
- ½ cup plain breadcrumbs
- oil for misting or cooking spray

Directions:

1. Rinse scallops and remove the tough side muscle. Sprinkle to taste with salt and pepper.
2. Beat eggs together in a shallow dish. Place flour in a second shallow dish and breadcrumbs in a third.
3. Preheat air fryer to 390°F.
4. Dip scallops in flour, then eggs, and then roll in breadcrumbs. Mist with oil or cooking spray.
5. Place scallops in air fryer basket in a single layer, leaving some space between. You should be able to cook about a dozen at a time.
6. Cook at 390°F for 8 minutes, watching carefully so as not to overcook. Scallops are done when they turn opaque all the way through. They will feel slightly firm when pressed with tines of a fork.
7. Repeat step 6 to cook remaining scallops.

Thyme Scallops

Servings: 1 | Cooking Time: 12 Minutes

Ingredients:

- 1 lb. scallops
- Salt and pepper
- ½ tbsp. butter
- ½ cup thyme, chopped

Directions:

1. Wash the scallops and dry them completely. Season with pepper and salt, then set aside while you prepare the pan.
2. Grease a foil pan in several spots with the butter and cover the bottom with the thyme. Place the scallops on top.
3. Pre-heat the fryer at 400°F and set the rack inside.
4. Place the foil pan on the rack and allow to cook for seven minutes.
5. Take care when removing the pan from the fryer and transfer the scallops to a serving dish. Spoon any remaining butter in the pan over the fish and enjoy.

Almond Topped Trout

Servings: 4 | Cooking Time: 20 Minutes

Ingredients:
- 4 trout fillets
- 2 tbsp olive oil
- Salt and pepper to taste
- 2 garlic cloves, sliced
- 1 lemon, sliced
- 1 tbsp flaked almonds

Directions:

1. Preheat air fryer to 380°F. Lightly brush each fillet with olive oil on both sides and season with salt and pepper. Put the fillets in a single layer in the frying basket. Put the sliced garlic over the tops of the trout fillets, then top with lemon slices and cook for 12-15 minutes. Serve topped with flaked almonds and enjoy!

Fried Catfish Fillets

Servings:2 | Cooking Time: 40 Minutes

Ingredients:
- 3 tbsp breadcrumbs
- 1 tsp cayenne pepper
- 1 tsp dry fish seasoning, of choice
- 2 sprigs parsley, chopped
- Salt to taste, optional
- Cooking spray

Directions:

1. Preheat air fryer to 400°F. Pour all the dry ingredients, except the parsley, in a zipper bag. Pat dry and add the fish pieces. Close the bag and shake to coat the fish well. Do this with one fish piece at a time.
2. Lightly spray the fish with olive oil. Arrange them in the fryer basket, one at a time depending on the size of the fish. Close the air fryer and cook for 10 minutes. Flip the fish and cook further for 10 minutes. For extra crispiness, cook for 3 more minutes. Garnish with parsley and serve.

Chili Blackened Shrimp

Servings: 4 | Cooking Time: 15 Minutes

Ingredients:
- 1 lb peeled shrimp, deveined
- 1 tsp paprika
- ½ tsp dried dill
- ½ tsp red chili flakes
- ½ lemon, juiced
- Salt and pepper to taste

Directions:

1. Preheat air fryer to 400°F. In a resealable bag, add shrimp, paprika, dill, red chili flakes, lemon juice, salt and pepper. Seal and shake well. Place the shrimp in the greased frying basket and Air Fry for 7-8 minutes, shaking the basket once until blackened. Let cool slightly and serve.

Sesame Tuna Steak

Servings: 2 | Cooking Time: 12 Minutes

Ingredients:

- 1 tbsp. coconut oil, melted
- 2 x 6-oz. tuna steaks
- ½ tsp. garlic powder
- 2 tsp. black sesame seeds
- 2 tsp. white sesame seeds

Directions:

1. Apply the coconut oil to the tuna steaks with a brunch, then season with garlic powder.
2. Combine the black and white sesame seeds. Embed them in the tuna steaks, covering the fish all over. Place the tuna into your air fryer.
3. Cook for eight minutes at 400°F, turning the fish halfway through.
4. The tuna steaks are ready when they have reached a temperature of 145°F. Serve straightaway.

Garlic-lemon Steamer Clams

Servings:2 | Cooking Time: 30 Minutes

Ingredients:

- 25 Manila clams, scrubbed
- 2 tbsp butter, melted
- 1 garlic clove, minced
- 2 lemon wedges

Directions:

1. Add the clams to a large bowl filled with water and let sit for 10 minutes. Drain. Pour more water and let sit for 10 more minutes. Drain. Preheat air fryer to 350°F. Place clams in the basket and Air Fry for 7 minutes. Discard any clams that don´t open. Remove clams from shells and place them into a large serving dish. Drizzle with melted butter and garlic and squeeze lemon on top. Serve.

Air Fried Cod With Basil Vinaigrette

Servings:4 | Cooking Time: 15 Minutes

Ingredients:

- ¼ cup olive oil
- 4 cod fillets
- A bunch of basil, torn
- Juice from 1 lemon, freshly squeezed
- Salt and pepper to taste

Directions:

1. Preheat the air fryer for 5 minutes.
2. Season the cod fillets with salt and pepper to taste.
3. Place in the air fryer and cook for 15 minutes at 350°F.
4. Meanwhile, mix the rest of the ingredients in a bowl and toss to combine.
5. Serve the air fried cod with the basil vinaigrette.

Shrimp Al Pesto

Servings: 4 | Cooking Time: 10 Minutes

Ingredients:
- 1 lb peeled shrimp, deveined
- ¼ cup pesto sauce
- 1 lime, sliced
- 2 cups cooked farro

Directions:

1. Preheat air fryer to 360°F. Coat the shrimp with the pesto sauce in a bowl. Put the shrimp in a single layer in the frying basket. Put the lime slices over the shrimp and Roast for 5 minutes. Remove lime and discard. Serve the shrimp over a bed of farro pilaf. Enjoy!

Seared Scallops In Beurre Blanc

Servings: 4 | Cooking Time: 15 Minutes

Ingredients:
- 1 lb sea scallops
- Salt and pepper to taste
- 2 tbsp butter, melted
- 1 lemon, zested and juiced
- 2 tbsp dry white wine

Directions:

1. Preheat the air fryer to 400°F. Sprinkle the scallops with salt and pepper, then set in a bowl. Combine the butter, lemon zest, lemon juice, and white wine in another bowl; mix well. Put the scallops in a baking pan and drizzle over them the mixture. Air Fry for 8-11 minutes, flipping over at about 5 minutes until opaque. Serve and enjoy!

Teriyaki Salmon

Servings:4 | Cooking Time: 27 Minutes

Ingredients:
- ½ cup teriyaki sauce
- ¼ teaspoon salt
- 1 teaspoon ground ginger
- ½ teaspoon garlic powder
- 4 boneless, skinless salmon fillets
- 2 tablespoons toasted sesame seeds

Directions:

1. In a large bowl, whisk teriyaki sauce, salt, ginger, and garlic powder. Add salmon to the bowl, being sure to coat each side with marinade. Cover and let marinate in refrigerator 15 minutes.
2. Preheat the air fryer to 375°F.
3. Spritz fillets with cooking spray and place in the air fryer basket. Cook 12 minutes, turning halfway through cooking time, until glaze has caramelized to a dark brown color, salmon flakes easily, and internal temperature reaches at least 145°F. Sprinkle sesame seeds on salmon and serve warm.

Maple Butter Salmon

Servings:4 | Cooking Time: 12 Minutes

Ingredients:

- 2 tablespoons salted butter, melted
- 1 teaspoon low-carb maple syrup
- 1 teaspoon yellow mustard
- 4 boneless, skinless salmon fillets
- ½ teaspoon salt

Directions:

1. In a small bowl, whisk together butter, syrup, and mustard. Brush ½ mixture over each fillet on both sides. Sprinkle fillets with salt on both sides.
2. Place salmon into ungreased air fryer basket. Adjust the temperature to 400°F and set the timer for 12 minutes. Halfway through cooking, brush fillets on both sides with remaining syrup mixture. Salmon will easily flake and have an internal temperature of at least 145°F when done. Serve warm.

Better Fish Sticks

Servings:3 | Cooking Time: 8 Minutes

Ingredients:

- ¾ cup Seasoned Italian-style dried bread crumbs (gluten-free, if a concern)
- 3 tablespoons (about ½ ounce) Finely grated Parmesan cheese
- 10 ounces Skinless cod fillets, cut lengthwise into 1-inch-wide pieces
- 3 tablespoons Regular or low-fat mayonnaise (not fat-free; gluten-free, if a concern)
- Vegetable oil spray

Directions:

1. Preheat the air fryer to 400°F.
2. Mix the bread crumbs and grated Parmesan in a shallow soup bowl or a small pie plate.
3. Smear the fish fillet sticks completely with the mayonnaise, then dip them one by one in the bread-crumb mixture, turning and pressing gently to make an even and thorough coating. Coat each stick on all sides with vegetable oil spray.
4. Set the fish sticks in the basket with at least ¼ inch between them. Air-fry undisturbed for 8 minutes, or until golden brown and crisp.
5. Use a nonstick-safe spatula to gently transfer them from the basket to a wire rack. Cool for only a minute or two before serving.

Crispy Sweet-and-sour Cod Fillets

Servings:3 | Cooking Time: 12 Minutes

Ingredients:

- 1½ cups Plain panko bread crumbs (gluten-free, if a concern)
- 2 tablespoons Regular or low-fat mayonnaise (not fat-free; gluten-free, if a concern)
- ¼ cup Sweet pickle relish
- 3 4- to 5-ounce skinless cod fillets

Directions:

1. Preheat the air fryer to 400°F.
2. Pour the bread crumbs into a shallow soup plate or a small pie plate. Mix the mayonnaise and relish in a small bowl until well combined. Smear this mixture all over the cod fillets. Set them in the crumbs and turn until evenly coated on all sides, even on the ends.
3. Set the coated cod fillets in the basket with as much air space between them as possible. They should not touch. Air-fry undisturbed for 12 minutes, or until browned and crisp.
4. Use a nonstick-safe spatula to transfer the cod pieces to a wire rack. Cool for only a minute or two before serving hot.

Miso Fish

Servings: 2 | Cooking Time: 10 Minutes

Ingredients:

- 2 cod fish fillets
- 1 tbsp garlic, chopped
- 2 tsp swerve
- 2 tbsp miso

Directions:

1. Add all ingredients to the zip-lock bag. Shake well place in the refrigerator for overnight.
2. Place marinated fish fillets into the air fryer basket and cook at 350°F for 10 minutes.
3. Serve and enjoy.

Crunchy And Buttery Cod With Ritz Cracker Crust

Servings: 2 | Cooking Time: 10 Minutes

Ingredients:
- 4 tablespoons butter, melted
- 8 to 10 RITZ crackers, crushed into crumbs
- 2 cod fillets
- salt and freshly ground black pepper
- 1 lemon

Directions:

1. Preheat the air fryer to 380°F.
2. Melt the butter in a small saucepan on the stovetop or in a microwavable dish in the microwave, and then transfer the butter to a shallow dish. Place the crushed RITZ crackers into a second shallow dish.
3. Season the fish fillets with salt and freshly ground black pepper. Dip them into the butter and then coat both sides with the RITZ crackers.
4. Place the fish into the air fryer basket and air-fry at 380°F for 10 minutes, flipping the fish over halfway through the cooking time.
5. Serve with a wedge of lemon to squeeze over the top.

Coconut Shrimp

Servings:4 | Cooking Time: 10 Minutes

Ingredients:
- 1 cup all-purpose flour
- 1 teaspoon salt
- 2 large eggs
- ½ cup panko bread crumbs
- 1 cup shredded unsweetened coconut flakes
- 1 pound large shrimp, peeled and deveined
- Cooking spray

Directions:

1. Preheat the air fryer to 375°F.
2. In a medium bowl, mix flour and salt. In a separate medium bowl, whisk eggs. In a third medium bowl, mix bread crumbs and coconut flakes.
3. Dredge shrimp first in flour mixture, shaking off excess, then in eggs, letting any additional egg drip off, and finally in bread crumb mixture. Spritz with cooking spray.
4. Place shrimp in the air fryer basket. Cook 10 minutes, turning and spritzing opposite side with cooking spray halfway through cooking, until insides are pearly white and opaque and internal temperature reaches at least 145°F. Serve warm.

Chapter 7 Vegetarians Recipes

Chapter 7 Vegetarians Recipes

Spaghetti Squash

Servings:4 | Cooking Time: 45 Minutes

Ingredients:

- 1 large spaghetti squash, halved lengthwise and seeded
- 1 teaspoon salt
- ½ teaspoon ground black pepper
- 1 teaspoon garlic powder
- 1 teaspoon dried parsley
- 2 tablespoons salted butter, melted

Directions:

1. Preheat the air fryer to 350°F.
2. Sprinkle squash with salt, pepper, garlic powder, and parsley. Spritz with cooking spray.
3. Place skin side down in the air fryer basket and cook 30 minutes.
4. Turn squash skin side up and cook an additional 15 minutes until fork-tender. You should be able to easily use a fork to scrape across the surface to separate the strands.
5. Place strands in a medium bowl, top with butter, and toss. Serve warm.

Sesame Seeds Bok Choy

Servings:4 | Cooking Time: 6 Minutes

Ingredients:

- 4 bunches baby bok choy, bottoms removed and leaves separated
- Olive oil cooking spray
- 1 teaspoon garlic powder
- 1 teaspoon sesame seeds

Directions:

1. Set the temperature of air fryer to 325°F.
2. Arrange bok choy leaves into the air fryer basket in a single layer.
3. Spray with the cooking spray and sprinkle with garlic powder.
4. Air fry for about 5-6 minutes, shaking after every 2 minutes.
5. Remove from air fryer and transfer the bok choy onto serving plates.
6. Garnish with sesame seeds and serve hot.

Caramelized Brussels Sprout

Servings:4 | Cooking Time:35 Minutes

Ingredients:

- 1 pound Brussels sprouts, trimmed and halved
- 4 teaspoons butter, melted
- Salt and black pepper, to taste

Directions:

1. Preheat the Air fryer to 400°F and grease an Air fryer basket.
2. Mix all the ingredients in a bowl and toss to coat well.
3. Arrange the Brussels sprouts in the Air fryer basket and cook for about 35 minutes.
4. Dish out and serve warm.

Spicy Roasted Cashew Nuts

Servings: 4 | Cooking Time: 20 Minutes

Ingredients:

- 1 cup whole cashews
- 1 teaspoon olive oil
- Salt and ground black pepper, to taste
- 1/2 teaspoon smoked paprika
- 1/2 teaspoon ancho chili powder

Directions:

1. Toss all ingredients in the mixing bowl.
2. Line the Air Fryer basket with baking parchment. Spread out the spiced cashews in a single layer in the basket.
3. Roast at 350°F for 6 to 8 minutes, shaking the basket once or twice. Work in batches. Enjoy!

Crispy Eggplant Rounds

Servings:4 | Cooking Time: 10 Minutes

Ingredients:

- 1 large eggplant, ends trimmed, cut into ½" slices
- ½ teaspoon salt
- 2 ounces Parmesan 100% cheese crisps, finely ground
- ½ teaspoon paprika
- ¼ teaspoon garlic powder
- 1 large egg

Directions:

1. Sprinkle eggplant rounds with salt. Place rounds on a kitchen towel for 30 minutes to draw out excess water. Pat rounds dry.
2. In a medium bowl, mix cheese crisps, paprika, and garlic powder. In a separate medium bowl, whisk egg. Dip each eggplant round in egg, then gently press into cheese crisps to coat both sides.
3. Place eggplant rounds into ungreased air fryer basket. Adjust the temperature to 400°F and set the timer for 10 minutes, turning rounds halfway through cooking. Eggplant will be golden and crispy when done. Serve warm.

Grilled 'n Glazed Strawberries

Servings:2 | Cooking Time: 20 Minutes

Ingredients:

- 1 tbsp honey
- 1 tsp lemon zest
- 1-lb large strawberries
- 3 tbsp melted butter
- Lemon wedges
- Pinch kosher salt

Directions:

1. Thread strawberries in 4 skewers.
2. In a small bowl, mix well remaining ingredients except for lemon wedges. Brush all over strawberries.
3. Place skewer on air fryer skewer rack.
4. For 10 minutes, cook on 360°F. Halfway through cooking time, brush with honey mixture and turnover skewer.
5. Serve and enjoy with a squeeze of lemon.

Cool Mini Zucchini's

Servings:4 | Cooking Time: 25 Minutes

Ingredients:

- 4 large eggs, beaten
- 1 medium zucchini, sliced
- 4 ounces feta cheese, drained and crumbled
- 2 tbsp fresh dill, chopped
- Cooking spray
- Salt and pepper as needed

Directions:

1. Preheat the air fryer to 360°F, and un a bowl, add the beaten eggs and season with salt and pepper.
2. Stir in zucchini, dill and feta cheese. Grease 8 muffin tins with cooking spray. Roll pastry and arrange them to cover the sides of the muffin tins. Divide the egg mixture evenly between the holes. Place the prepared tins in your air fryer and cook for 15 minutes. Serve and enjoy!

Home-style Cinnamon Rolls

Servings: 4 | Cooking Time: 40 Minutes

Ingredients:

- ½ pizza dough
- 1/3 cup dark brown sugar
- ¼ cup butter, softened
- ½ tsp ground cinnamon

Directions:

1. Preheat air fryer to 360°F. Roll out the dough into a rectangle. Using a knife, spread the brown sugar and butter, covering all the edges, and sprinkle with cinnamon. Fold the long side of the dough into a log, then cut it into 8 equal pieces, avoiding compression. Place the rolls, spiral-side up, onto a parchment-lined sheet. Let rise for 20 minutes. Grease the rolls with cooking spray and Bake for 8 minutes until golden brown. Serve right away.

Twice-baked Broccoli-cheddar Potatoes

Servings:4 | Cooking Time: 35 Minutes

Ingredients:

- 4 large russet potatoes
- 2 tablespoons plus 2 teaspoons ranch dressing
- 1 teaspoon salt
- ½ teaspoon ground black pepper
- ¼ cup chopped cooked broccoli florets
- 1 cup shredded sharp Cheddar cheese

Directions:

1. Preheat the air fryer to 400°F.
2. Using a fork, poke several holes in potatoes. Place in the air fryer basket and cook 30 minutes until fork-tender.
3. Once potatoes are cool enough to handle, slice lengthwise and scoop out the cooked potato into a large bowl, being careful to maintain the structural integrity of potato skins. Add ranch dressing, salt, pepper, broccoli, and Cheddar to potato flesh and stir until well combined.
4. Scoop potato mixture back into potato skins and return to the air fryer basket. Cook an additional 5 minutes until cheese is melted. Serve warm.

Two-cheese Grilled Sandwiches

Servings: 2 | Cooking Time: 30 Minutes

Ingredients:

- 4 sourdough bread slices
- 2 cheddar cheese slices
- 2 Swiss cheese slices
- 1 tbsp butter
- 2 dill pickles, sliced

Directions:

1. Preheat air fryer to 360°F. Smear both sides of the sourdough bread with butter and place them in the frying basket. Toast the bread for 6 minutes, flipping once.
2. Divide the cheddar cheese between 2 of the bread slices. Cover the remaining 2 bread slices with Swiss cheese slices. Bake for 10 more minutes until the cheeses have melted and lightly bubbled and the bread has golden brown. Set the cheddar-covered bread slices on a serving plate, cover with pickles, and top each with the Swiss-covered slices. Serve and enjoy!

Zucchini Fritters

Servings:4 | Cooking Time: 12 Minutes

Ingredients:

- 1½ medium zucchini, trimmed and grated
- ½ teaspoon salt, divided
- 1 large egg, whisked
- ¼ teaspoon garlic powder
- ¼ cup grated Parmesan cheese

Directions:

1. Place grated zucchini on a kitchen towel and sprinkle with ¼ teaspoon salt. Wrap in towel and let sit 30 minutes, then wring out as much excess moisture as possible.
2. Place zucchini into a large bowl and mix with egg, remaining salt, garlic powder, and Parmesan. Cut a piece of parchment to fit air fryer basket. Divide mixture into four mounds, about ⅓ cup each, and press out into 4" rounds on ungreased parchment.
3. Place parchment with rounds into air fryer basket. Adjust the temperature to 400°F and set the timer for 12 minutes, turning fritters halfway through cooking. Fritters will be crispy on the edges and tender but firm in the center when done. Serve warm.

Cinnamon Sugar Tortilla Chips

Servings: 4 | Cooking Time: 20 Minutes

Ingredients:

- 4 flour tortillas
- 1/4 cup vegan margarine, melted
- 1 ½ tablespoons ground cinnamon
- 1/4 cup caster sugar

Directions:

1. Slice each tortilla into eight slices. Brush the tortilla pieces with the melted margarine.
2. In a mixing bowl, thoroughly combine the cinnamon and sugar. Toss the cinnamon mixture with the tortillas.
3. Transfer to the cooking basket and cook at 360°F for 8 minutes or until lightly golden. Work in batches.
4. They will crisp up as they cool. Serve and enjoy!

Vegetable Burgers

Servings:4 | Cooking Time: 12 Minutes

Ingredients:
- 8 ounces cremini mushrooms
- 2 large egg yolks
- ½ medium zucchini, trimmed and chopped
- ¼ cup peeled and chopped yellow onion
- 1 clove garlic, peeled and finely minced
- ½ teaspoon salt
- ¼ teaspoon ground black pepper

Directions:
1. Place all ingredients into a food processor and pulse twenty times until finely chopped and combined.
2. Separate mixture into four equal sections and press each into a burger shape. Place burgers into ungreased air fryer basket. Adjust the temperature to 375°F and set the timer for 12 minutes, turning burgers halfway through cooking. Burgers will be browned and firm when done.
3. Place burgers on a large plate and let cool 5 minutes before serving.

Crispy Apple Fries With Caramel Sauce

Servings: 4 | Cooking Time: 15 Minutes

Ingredients:
- 4 medium apples, cored
- ¼ tsp cinnamon
- ¼ tsp nutmeg
- 1 cup caramel sauce

Directions:
1. Preheat air fryer to 350°F. Slice the apples to a 1/3-inch thickness for a crunchy chip. Place in a large bowl and sprinkle with cinnamon and nutmeg. Place the slices in the air fryer basket. Bake for 6 minutes. Shake the basket, then cook for another 4 minutes or until crunchy. Serve drizzled with caramel sauce and enjoy!

Brussels Sprouts With Balsamic Oil

Servings:4 | Cooking Time: 15 Minutes

Ingredients:
- ¼ teaspoon salt
- 1 tablespoon balsamic vinegar
- 2 cups Brussels sprouts, halved
- 2 tablespoons olive oil

Directions:
1. Preheat the air fryer for 5 minutes.
2. Mix all ingredients in a bowl until the zucchini fries are well coated.
3. Place in the air fryer basket.
4. Close and cook for 15 minutes for 350°F.

Broccoli & Parmesan Dish

Servings:4 | Cooking Time: 25 Minutes

Ingredients:

- 1 tbsp olive oil
- 1 lemon, Juiced
- Salt and pepper to taste
- 1-ounce Parmesan cheese, grated

Directions:

1. In a bowl, mix all ingredients. Add the mixture to your air fryer and cook for 20 minutes at 360°F. Serve.

Broccoli With Cauliflower

Servings:4 | Cooking Time:20 Minutes

Ingredients:

- 1½ cups broccoli, cut into 1-inch pieces
- 1½ cups cauliflower, cut into 1-inch pieces
- 1 tablespoon olive oil
- Salt, as required

Directions:

1. Preheat the Air fryer to 375°F and grease an Air fryer basket.
2. Mix the vegetables, olive oil, and salt in a bowl and toss to coat well.
3. Arrange the veggie mixture in the Air fryer basket and cook for about 20 minutes, tossing once in between.
4. Dish out in a bowl and serve hot.

Crispy Shawarma Broccoli

Servings: 4 | Cooking Time: 25 Minutes

Ingredients:

- 1 pound broccoli, steamed and drained
- 2 tablespoons canola oil
- 1 teaspoon cayenne pepper
- 1 teaspoon sea salt
- 1 tablespoon Shawarma spice blend

Directions:

1. Toss all ingredients in a mixing bowl.
2. Roast in the preheated Air Fryer at 380°F for 10 minutes, shaking the basket halfway through the cooking time.
3. Work in batches. Bon appétit!

Zucchini Gratin

Servings: 2 | Cooking Time: 15 Minutes

Ingredients:

- 5 oz. parmesan cheese, shredded
- 1 tbsp. coconut flour
- 1 tbsp. dried parsley
- 2 zucchinis
- 1 tsp. butter, melted

Directions:

1. Mix the parmesan and coconut flour together in a bowl, seasoning with parsley to taste.
2. Cut the zucchini in half lengthwise and chop the halves into four slices.
3. Pre-heat the fryer at 400°F.
4. Pour the melted butter over the zucchini and then dip the zucchini into the parmesan-flour mixture, coating it all over. Cook the zucchini in the fryer for thirteen minutes.

Caramelized Carrots

Servings:3 | Cooking Time:15 Minutes

Ingredients:

- 1 small bag baby carrots
- ½ cup butter, melted
- ½ cup brown sugar

Directions:

1. Preheat the Air fryer to 400°F and grease an Air fryer basket.
2. Mix the butter and brown sugar in a bowl.
3. Add the carrots and toss to coat well.
4. Arrange the carrots in the Air fryer basket and cook for about 15 minutes.
5. Dish out and serve warm.

Chapter 8 Vegetable Side Dishes Recipes

Chapter 8 Vegetable Side Dishes Recipes

Cheesy Vegetarian Lasagna

Servings: 4 | Cooking Time: 40 Minutes

Ingredients:

- 1 ¼ cups shredded Italian-blend cheese, divided
- ½ cup grated vegetarian Parmesan cheese, divided
- ½ cup full-fat ricotta cheese
- ½ teaspoon salt
- ¼ teaspoon ground black pepper
- 2 cups tomato pasta sauce, divided
- 5 no-boil lasagna noodles

Directions:

1. Preheat the air fryer to 360°F. Spritz a 6" round baking pan with cooking spray.
2. In a medium bowl, mix 1 cup Italian-blend cheese, ¼ cup Parmesan, ricotta, salt, and pepper.
3. Pour ½ cup pasta sauce into the bottom of the prepared pan. Break the noodles into pieces to fit the pan. Place a layer of noodles into the pan.
4. Separate ricotta mixture into three portions. Spread one-third of the mixture over noodles in the pan. Pour ½ cup pasta sauce over ricotta mixture. Repeat layers of noodles, cheese mixture, and pasta sauce twice more until all ingredients are used, topping the final layer with remaining Italian-blend cheese.
5. Cover pan tightly with foil, being sure to tuck foil under the bottom of the pan to ensure the air fryer fan does not blow it off. Place in the air fryer basket. Cook 35 minutes, then remove foil and cook an additional 5 minutes until the top is golden brown and noodles are fork-tender.
6. Remove from the air fryer basket and top with remaining Parmesan and let cool 5 minutes before serving.

Macaroni And Cheese

Servings: 4 | Cooking Time: 25 Minutes

Ingredients:

- 1 ½ cups dry elbow macaroni
- 1 cup chicken broth
- ½ cup whole milk
- 2 tablespoons salted butter, melted
- 8 ounces sharp Cheddar cheese, shredded, divided
- ½ teaspoon ground black pepper

Directions:

1. Preheat the air fryer to 350°F.
2. In a 6" baking dish, combine macaroni, broth, milk, butter, half the Cheddar, and pepper. Stir to combine.
3. Place in the air fryer basket and cook 12 minutes.
4. Stir in remaining Cheddar, then return the basket to the air fryer and cook 13 additional minutes.
5. Stir macaroni and cheese until creamy. Let cool 10 minutes before serving.

Roman Artichokes

Servings: 4 | Cooking Time: 12 Minutes

Ingredients:

- 2 9-ounce box(es) frozen artichoke heart quarters, thawed
- 1½ tablespoons Olive oil
- 2 teaspoons Minced garlic
- 1 teaspoon Table salt
- Up to ½ teaspoon Red pepper flakes

Directions:

1. Preheat the air fryer to 400°F.
2. Gently toss the artichoke heart quarters, oil, garlic, salt, and red pepper flakes in a bowl until the quarters are well coated.
3. When the machine is at temperature, scrape the contents of the bowl into the basket. Spread the artichoke heart quarters out into as close to one layer as possible. Air-fry undisturbed for 8 minutes. Gently toss and rearrange the quarters so that any covered or touching parts are now exposed to the air currents, then air-fry undisturbed for 4 minutes more, until very crisp.
4. Gently pour the contents of the basket onto a wire rack. Cool for a few minutes before serving.

Cheesy Loaded Broccoli

Servings:2 | Cooking Time: 10 Minutes

Ingredients:

- 3 cups fresh broccoli florets
- 1 tablespoon coconut oil
- ¼ teaspoon salt
- ½ cup shredded sharp Cheddar cheese
- ¼ cup sour cream
- 4 slices cooked sugar-free bacon, crumbled
- 1 medium scallion, trimmed and sliced on the bias

Directions:

1. Place broccoli into ungreased air fryer basket, drizzle with coconut oil, and sprinkle with salt. Adjust the temperature to 350°F and set the timer for 8 minutes. Shake basket three times during cooking to avoid burned spots.
2. When timer beeps, sprinkle broccoli with Cheddar and set the timer for 2 additional minutes. When done, cheese will be melted and broccoli will be tender.
3. Serve warm in a large serving dish, topped with sour cream, crumbled bacon, and scallion slices.

Roasted Cauliflower With Garlic And Capers

Servings: 3 | Cooking Time: 10 Minutes

Ingredients:

- 3 cups 1-inch cauliflower florets
- 2 tablespoons Olive oil
- 1½ tablespoons Drained and rinsed capers, chopped
- 2 teaspoons Minced garlic
- ¼ teaspoon Table salt
- Up to ¼ teaspoon Red pepper flakes

Directions:

1. Preheat the air fryer to 375°F .
2. Stir the cauliflower florets, olive oil, capers, garlic, salt, and red pepper flakes in a large bowl until the florets are evenly coated.
3. When the machine is at temperature, put the florets in the basket, spreading them out to as close to one layer as you can. Air-fry for 10 minutes, tossing once to get any covered pieces exposed to the air currents, until tender and lightly browned.
4. Dump the contents of the basket into a serving bowl or onto a serving platter. Cool for a minute or two before serving.

Perfect French Fries

Servings: 3 | Cooking Time: 37 Minutes

Ingredients:

- 1 pound Large russet potato(es)
- Vegetable oil or olive oil spray
- ½ teaspoon Table salt

Directions:

1. Cut each potato lengthwise into ¼-inch-thick slices. Cut each of these lengthwise into ¼-inch-thick matchsticks.
2. Set the potato matchsticks in a big bowl of cool water and soak for 5 minutes. Drain in a colander set in the sink, then spread the matchsticks out on paper towels and dry them very well.
3. Preheat the air fryer to 225°F.
4. When the machine is at temperature, arrange the matchsticks in an even layer in the basket. Air-fry for 20 minutes, tossing and rearranging the fries twice.
5. Pour the contents of the basket into a big bowl. Increase the air fryer's temperature to 325°F.
6. Generously coat the fries with vegetable or olive oil spray. Toss well, then coat them again to make sure they're covered on all sides, tossing a couple of times to make sure.
7. When the machine is at temperature, pour the fries into the basket and air-fry for 12 minutes, tossing and rearranging the fries at least twice.
8. Increase the machine's temperature to 375°F. Air-fry for 5 minutes more, tossing and rearranging the fries at least twice to keep them from burning and to make sure they all get an even measure of the heat, until brown and crisp.
9. Pour the contents of the basket into a serving bowl. Toss the fries with the salt and serve hot.

Cheesy Texas Toast

Servings: 2 | Cooking Time: 4 Minutes

Ingredients:

- 2 1-inch-thick slice(s) Italian bread
- 4 teaspoons Softened butter
- 2 teaspoons Minced garlic
- ¼ cup (about ¾ ounce) Finely grated Parmesan cheese

Directions:

1. Preheat the air fryer to 400°F.
2. Spread one side of a slice of bread with 2 teaspoons butter. Sprinkle with 1 teaspoon minced garlic, followed by 2 tablespoons grated cheese. Repeat this process if you're making one or more additional toasts.
3. When the machine is at temperature, put the bread slice(s) cheese side up in the basket (with as much air space between them as possible if you're making more than one). Air-fry undisturbed for 4 minutes, or until browned and crunchy.
4. Use a nonstick-safe spatula to transfer the toasts cheese side up to a wire rack. Cool for 5 minutes before serving.

Asparagus Wrapped In Pancetta

Servings: 4 | Cooking Time: 30 Minutes

Ingredients:

- 20 asparagus trimmed
- Salt and pepper pepper
- 4 pancetta slices
- 1 tbsp fresh sage, chopped

Directions:

1. Sprinkle the asparagus with fresh sage, salt and pepper. Toss to coat. Make 4 bundles of 5 spears by wrapping the center of the bunch with one slice of pancetta.
2. Preheat air fryer to 400°F. Put the bundles in the greased frying basket and Air Fry for 8-10 minutes or until the pancetta is brown and the asparagus are starting to char on the edges. Serve immediately.

"Faux-tato" Hash

Servings:4 | Cooking Time: 12 Minutes

Ingredients:

- 1 pound radishes, ends removed, quartered
- ¼ medium yellow onion, peeled and diced
- ½ medium green bell pepper, seeded and chopped
- 2 tablespoons salted butter, melted
- ½ teaspoon garlic powder
- ¼ teaspoon ground black pepper

Directions:

1. In a large bowl, combine radishes, onion, and bell pepper. Toss with butter.
2. Sprinkle garlic powder and black pepper over mixture in bowl, then spoon into ungreased air fryer basket.
3. Adjust the temperature to 320°F and set the timer for 12 minutes. Shake basket halfway through cooking. Radishes will be tender when done. Serve warm.

Beet Fries

Ingredients:

- 3 6-ounce red beets
- Vegetable oil spray
- To taste Coarse sea salt or kosher salt

Directions:

1. Preheat the air fryer to 375°F.
2. Remove the stems from the beets and peel them with a knife or vegetable peeler. Slice them into ½-inch-thick circles. Lay these flat on a cutting board and slice them into ½-inch-thick sticks. Generously coat the sticks on all sides with vegetable oil spray.
3. When the machine is at temperature, drop them into the basket, shake the basket to even the sticks out into as close to one layer as possible, and air-fry for 20 minutes, tossing and rearranging the beet matchsticks every 5 minutes, or until brown and even crisp at the ends. If the machine is at 360°F, you may need to add 2 minutes to the cooking time.
4. Pour the fries into a big bowl, add the salt, toss well, and serve warm.

Dauphinoise (potatoes Au Gratin)

Servings: 4 | Cooking Time: 30 Minutes

Ingredients:

- ½ cup grated cheddar cheese
- 3 peeled potatoes, sliced
- ½ cup milk
- ½ cup heavy cream
- Salt and pepper to taste
- 1 tsp ground nutmeg

Directions:

1. Preheat air fryer to 350°F. Place the milk, heavy cream, salt, pepper, and nutmeg in a bowl and mix well. Dip in the potato slices and arrange on a baking dish. Spoon the remaining mixture over the potatoes. Scatter the grated cheddar cheese on top. Place the baking dish in the air fryer and Bake for 20 minutes. Serve warm and enjoy!

Cheesy Baked Asparagus

Servings:4 | Cooking Time: 18 Minutes

Ingredients:
- ½ cup heavy whipping cream
- ½ cup grated Parmesan cheese
- 2 ounces cream cheese, softened
- 1 pound asparagus, ends trimmed, chopped into 1" pieces
- ¼ teaspoon salt
- ¼ teaspoon ground black pepper

Directions:

1. In a medium bowl, whisk together heavy cream, Parmesan, and cream cheese until combined.
2. Place asparagus into an ungreased 6" round nonstick baking dish. Pour cheese mixture over top and sprinkle with salt and pepper.
3. Place dish into air fryer basket. Adjust the temperature to 350°F and set the timer for 18 minutes. Asparagus will be tender when done. Serve warm.

Flatbread Dippers

Servings:12 | Cooking Time: 8 Minutes

Ingredients:
- 1 cup shredded mozzarella cheese
- 1 ounce cream cheese, broken into small pieces
- ½ cup blanched finely ground almond flour

Directions:

1. Place mozzarella into a large microwave-safe bowl. Add cream cheese pieces. Microwave on high 60 seconds, then stir to combine. Add flour and stir until a soft ball of dough forms.
2. Cut dough ball into two equal pieces. Cut a piece of parchment to fit into air fryer basket. Press each dough piece into a 5" round on ungreased parchment.
3. Place parchment with dough into air fryer basket. Adjust the temperature to 350°F and set the timer for 8 minutes. Carefully flip the flatbread over halfway through cooking. Flatbread will be golden brown when done.
4. Let flatbread cool 5 minutes, then slice each round into six triangles. Serve warm.

Twice-baked Potatoes With Pancetta

Servings: 5 | Cooking Time: 30 Minutes

Ingredients:

- 2 teaspoons canola oil
- 5 large russet potatoes, peeled
- Sea salt and ground black pepper, to taste
- 5 slices pancetta, chopped
- 5 tablespoons Swiss cheese, shredded

Directions:

1. Start by preheating your Air Fryer to 360 °F.
2. Drizzle the canola oil all over the potatoes. Place the potatoes in the Air Fryer basket and cook approximately 20 minutes, shaking the basket periodically.
3. Lightly crush the potatoes to split and season them with salt and ground black pepper. Add the pancetta and cheese.
4. Place in the preheated Air Fryer and bake an additional 5 minutes or until cheese has melted. Bon appétit!

Roasted Broccoli Salad

Servings:4 | Cooking Time: 7 Minutes

Ingredients:

- 2 cups fresh broccoli florets, chopped
- 1 tablespoon olive oil
- ¼ teaspoon salt
- ⅛ teaspoon ground black pepper
- ¼ cup lemon juice, divided
- ¼ cup shredded Parmesan cheese
- ¼ cup sliced roasted almonds

Directions:

1. In a large bowl, toss broccoli and olive oil together. Sprinkle with salt and pepper, then drizzle with 2 tablespoons lemon juice.
2. Place broccoli into ungreased air fryer basket. Adjust the temperature to 350°F and set the timer for 7 minutes, shaking the basket halfway through cooking. Broccoli will be golden on the edges when done.
3. Place broccoli into a large serving bowl and drizzle with remaining lemon juice. Sprinkle with Parmesan and almonds. Serve warm.

Mini Hasselback Potatoes

Servings: 4 | Cooking Time: 25 Minutes

Ingredients:

- 1½ pounds baby Yukon Gold potatoes
- 5 tablespoons butter, cut into very thin slices
- salt and freshly ground black pepper
- 1 tablespoon vegetable oil
- ¼ cup grated Parmesan cheese (optional)
- chopped fresh parsley or chives

Directions:

1. Preheat the air fryer to 400°F.
2. Make six to eight deep vertical slits across the top of each potato about three quarters of the way down. Make sure the slits are deep enough to allow the slices to spread apart a little, but don't cut all the way through the potato. Place a thin slice of butter between each of the slices and season generously with salt and pepper.
3. Transfer the potatoes to the air fryer basket. Pack them in next to each other. It's alright if some of the potatoes sit on top or rest on another potato. Air-fry for 20 minutes.
4. Spray or brush the potatoes with a little vegetable oil and sprinkle the Parmesan cheese on top. Air-fry for an additional 5 minutes. Garnish with chopped parsley or chives and serve hot.

Yeast Rolls

Servings:16 | Cooking Time: 1 Hour 10 Minutes

Ingredients:

- 4 tablespoons salted butter
- ¼ cup granulated sugar
- 1 cup hot water
- 1 tablespoon quick-rise yeast
- 1 large egg
- 1 teaspoon salt
- 2 ½ cups all-purpose flour, divided
- Cooking spray

Directions:

1. In a microwave-safe bowl, microwave butter 30 seconds until melted. Pour 2 tablespoons of butter into a large bowl. Add sugar, hot water, and yeast. Mix until yeast is dissolved.
2. Using a rubber spatula, mix in egg, salt, and 2 ¼ cups flour. Dough will be very sticky.
3. Cover bowl with plastic wrap and let rise in a warm place 1 hour.
4. Sprinkle remaining ¼ cup flour on dough and turn onto a lightly floured surface. Knead 2 minutes, then cut into sixteen even pieces.
5. Preheat the air fryer to 350°F. Spray a 6" round cake pan with cooking spray.
6. Sprinkle each roll with flour and arrange in pan. Brush with remaining melted butter. Place pan in the air fryer basket and cook 10 minutes until fluffy and golden on top. Serve warm.

Mashed Potato Pancakes

Servings: 6 | Cooking Time: 10 Minutes

Ingredients:

- 2 cups leftover mashed potatoes
- ½ cup grated cheddar cheese
- ¼ cup thinly sliced green onions
- ½ teaspoon salt
- ¼ teaspoon black pepper
- 1 cup breadcrumbs

Directions:

1. Preheat the air fryer to 380°F.
2. In a large bowl, mix together the potatoes, cheese, and onions. Using a ¼ cup measuring cup, measure out 6 patties. Form the potatoes into ½-inch thick patties. Season the patties with salt and pepper on both sides.
3. In a small bowl, place the breadcrumbs. Gently press the potato pancakes into the breadcrumbs.
4. Place the potato pancakes into the air fryer basket and spray with cooking spray. Cook for 5 minutes, turn the pancakes over, and cook another 3 to 5 minutes or until golden brown on the outside and cooked through on the inside.

Fried Corn On The Cob

Servings: 2 | Cooking Time: 10 Minutes

Ingredients:

- 1½ tablespoons Regular or low-fat mayonnaise (not fat-free; gluten-free, if a concern)
- 1½ teaspoons Minced garlic
- ¼ teaspoon Table salt
- ¾ cup Plain panko bread crumbs (gluten-free, if a concern)
- 3 4-inch lengths husked and de-silked corn on the cob
- Vegetable oil spray

Directions:

1. Preheat the air fryer to 400°F.
2. Stir the mayonnaise, garlic, and salt in a small bowl until well combined. Spread the panko on a dinner plate.
3. Brush the mayonnaise mixture over the kernels of a piece of corn on the cob. Set the corn in the bread crumbs, then roll, pressing gently, to coat it. Lightly coat with vegetable oil spray. Set it aside, then coat the remaining piece(s) of corn in the same way.
4. Set the coated corn on the cob in the basket with as much air space between the pieces as possible. Air-fry undisturbed for 10 minutes, or until brown and crisp along the coating.
5. Use kitchen tongs to gently transfer the pieces of corn to a wire rack. Cool for 5 minutes before serving.

Savory Brussels Sprouts

Servings: 4 | Cooking Time: 15 Minutes

Ingredients:

- 1 lb Brussels sprouts, quartered
- 2 tbsp balsamic vinegar
- 1 tbsp olive oil
- 1 tbsp honey
- Salt and pepper to taste
- 1 ½ tbsp lime juice
- Parsley for sprinkling

Directions:

1. Preheat air fryer at 350ºF. Combine all ingredients in a bowl. Transfer them to the frying basket. Air Fry for 10 minutes, tossing once. Top with lime juice and parsley.

Simple Zucchini Ribbons

Servings:4 | Cooking Time: 15 Minutes

Ingredients:

- 2 zucchini
- 2 tsp butter, melted
- ¼ tsp garlic powder
- ¼ tsp chili flakes
- 8 cherry tomatoes, halved
- Salt and pepper to taste

Directions:

1. Preheat air fryer to 275ºF. Cut the zucchini into ribbons with a vegetable peeler. Mix them with butter, garlic, chili flakes, salt, and pepper in a bowl. Transfer to the frying basket and Air Fry for 2 minutes. Toss and add the cherry tomatoes. Cook for another 2 minutes. Serve.

Swiss Chard Mix

Servings: 5 | Cooking Time: 15 Minutes

Ingredients:

- 7 oz Swiss chard, chopped
- 4 oz Swiss cheese, grated
- 4 teaspoons almond flour
- ½ cup heavy cream
- ½ teaspoon ground black pepper

Directions:

1. Mix up Swiss chard and Swiss cheese. Add almond flour, heavy cream, and ground black pepper. Stir the mixture until homogenous. After this, transfer it in 5 small ramekins. Preheat the air fryer to 365ºF. Place the ramekins with gratin in the air fryer basket and cook them for 15 minutes.

Chapter 9 Desserts And Sweets Recipes

Chapter 9 Desserts And Sweets Recipes

Orange Marmalade

Servings: 4 | Cooking Time: 20 Minutes

Ingredients:

- 4 oranges, peeled and chopped
- 3 cups sugar
- 1½ cups water

Directions:

1. In a pan that fits your air fryer, mix the oranges with the sugar and the water; stir.
2. Place the pan in the fryer and cook at 340°F for 20 minutes.
3. Stir well, divide into cups, refrigerate, and serve cold.

Oreo-coated Peanut Butter Cups

Servings:8 | Cooking Time: 4 Minutes

Ingredients:

- 8 Standard ¾-ounce peanut butter cups, frozen
- ⅓ cup All-purpose flour
- 2 Large egg white(s), beaten until foamy
- 16 Oreos or other creme-filled chocolate sandwich cookies, ground to crumbs in a food processor
- Vegetable oil spray

Directions:

1. Set up and fill three shallow soup plates or small pie plates on your counter: one for the flour, one for the beaten egg white(s), and one for the cookie crumbs.
2. Dip a frozen peanut butter cup in the flour, turning it to coat all sides. Shake off any excess, then set it in the beaten egg white(s). Turn it to coat all sides, then let any excess egg white slip back into the rest. Set the candy bar in the cookie crumbs. Turn to coat on all parts, even the sides. Dip the peanut butter cup back in the egg white(s) as before, then into the cookie crumbs as before, making sure you have a solid, even coating all around the cup. Set aside while you dip and coat the remaining cups.
3. When all the peanut butter cups are dipped and coated, lightly coat them on all sides with the vegetable oil spray. Set them on a plate and freeze while the air fryer heats.
4. Preheat the air fryer to 400°F.
5. Set the dipped cups wider side up in the basket with as much air space between them as possible. Air-fry undisturbed for 4 minutes, or until they feel soft but the coating is set.
6. Turn off the machine and remove the basket from it. Set aside the basket with the fried cups for 10 minutes. Use a non-stick-safe spatula to transfer the fried cups to a wire rack. Cool for at least another 5 minutes before serving.

Easy Mug Brownie

Servings: 1 | Cooking Time: 10 Minutes

Ingredients:

- 1 scoop chocolate protein powder
- 1 tbsp cocoa powder
- 1/2 tsp baking powder
- 1/4 cup unsweetened almond milk

Directions:

1. Add baking powder, protein powder, and cocoa powder in a mug and mix well.
2. Add milk in a mug and stir well.
3. Place the mug in the air fryer and cook at 390°F for 10 minutes.
4. Serve and enjoy.

Banana And Rice Pudding

Servings: 6 | Cooking Time: 20 Minutes

Ingredients:

- 1 cup brown rice
- 3 cups milk
- 2 bananas, peeled and mashed
- ½ cup maple syrup
- 1 teaspoon vanilla extract

Directions:

1. Place all the ingredients in a pan that fits your air fryer; stir well.
2. Put the pan in the fryer and cook at 360°F for 20 minutes.
3. Stir the pudding, divide into cups, refrigerate, and serve cold.

Cinnamon-sugar Pretzel Bites

Servings:4 | Cooking Time: 1 Hour 10 Minutes

Ingredients:
- 1 cup all-purpose flour
- 1 teaspoon quick-rise yeast
- 2 tablespoons granulated sugar, divided
- ¼ teaspoon salt
- 1 tablespoon olive oil
- ⅓ cup warm water
- 2 teaspoons baking soda
- 1 teaspoon ground cinnamon
- Cooking spray

Directions:

1. In a large bowl, mix flour, yeast, 2 teaspoons sugar, and salt until combined.
2. Pour in oil and water and stir until a dough begins to form and pull away from the edges of the bowl. Remove dough from the bowl and transfer to a lightly floured surface. Knead 10 minutes until dough is mostly smooth.
3. Spritz dough with cooking spray and place into a large clean bowl. Cover with plastic wrap and let rise 1 hour.
4. Preheat the air fryer to 400°F.
5. Press dough into a 6" × 4" rectangle. Cut dough into twenty-four even pieces.
6. Fill a medium saucepan over medium-high heat halfway with water and bring to a boil. Add baking soda and let it boil 1 minute, then add pretzel bites. You may need to work in batches. Cook 45 seconds, then remove from water and drain. They will be puffy but should have mostly maintained their shape.
7. Spritz pretzel bites with cooking spray. Place in the air fryer basket and cook 5 minutes until golden brown.
8. In a small bowl, mix remaining sugar and cinnamon. When pretzel bites are done cooking, immediately toss in cinnamon and sugar mixture and serve.

Chocolate Chip Cookie Cake

Servings:8 | Cooking Time: 15 Minutes

Ingredients:
- 4 tablespoons salted butter, melted
- ⅓ cup granular brown erythritol
- 1 large egg
- ½ teaspoon vanilla extract
- 1 cup blanched finely ground almond flour
- ½ teaspoon baking powder
- ¼ cup low-carb chocolate chips

Directions:

1. In a large bowl, whisk together butter, erythritol, egg, and vanilla. Add flour and baking powder, and stir until combined.
2. Fold in chocolate chips, then spoon batter into an ungreased 6" round nonstick baking dish.
3. Place dish into air fryer basket. Adjust the temperature to 300°F and set the timer for 15 minutes. When edges are browned, cookie cake will be done.
4. Slice and serve warm.

Easy Keto Danish

Servings:6 | Cooking Time: 12 Minutes

Ingredients:

- 1½ cups shredded mozzarella cheese
- ½ cup blanched finely ground almond flour
- 3 ounces cream cheese, divided
- ¼ cup confectioners' erythritol
- 1 tablespoon lemon juice

Directions:

1. Place mozzarella, flour, and 1 ounce cream cheese in a large microwave-safe bowl. Microwave on high 45 seconds, then stir with a fork until a soft dough forms.
2. Separate dough into six equal sections and press each in a single layer into an ungreased 4" × 4" square nonstick baking dish to form six even squares that touch.
3. In a small bowl, mix remaining cream cheese, erythritol, and lemon juice. Place 1 tablespoon mixture in center of each piece of dough in baking dish. Fold all four corners of each dough piece halfway to center to reach cream cheese mixture.
4. Place dish into air fryer. Adjust the temperature to 320°F and set the timer for 12 minutes. The center and edges will be browned when done. Let cool 10 minutes before serving.

Creamy Pudding

Servings: 6 | Cooking Time: 25 Minutes

Ingredients:

- 2 cups fresh cream
- 6 egg yolks, whisked
- 6 tablespoons white sugar
- Zest of 1 orange

Directions:

1. Combine all ingredients in a bowl and whisk well.
2. Divide the mixture between 6 small ramekins.
3. Place the ramekins in your air fryer and cook at 340°F for 25 minutes.
4. Place in the fridge for 1 hour before serving.

Pumpkin Pie–spiced Pork Rinds

Servings:4 | Cooking Time: 5 Minutes

Ingredients:

- 3 ounces plain pork rinds
- 2 tablespoons salted butter, melted
- 1 teaspoon pumpkin pie spice
- ¼ cup confectioners' erythritol

Directions:

1. In a large bowl, toss pork rinds in butter. Sprinkle with pumpkin pie spice, then toss to evenly coat.
2. Place pork rinds into ungreased air fryer basket. Adjust the temperature to 400°F and set the timer for 5 minutes. Pork rinds will be golden when done.
3. Transfer rinds to a medium serving bowl and sprinkle with erythritol. Serve immediately.

Delicious Spiced Apples

Servings: 6 | Cooking Time: 10 Minutes

Ingredients:

- 4 small apples, sliced
- 1 tsp apple pie spice
- 1/2 cup erythritol
- 2 tbsp coconut oil, melted

Directions:

1. Add apple slices in a mixing bowl and sprinkle sweetener, apple pie spice, and coconut oil over apple and toss to coat.
2. Transfer apple slices in air fryer dish. Place dish in air fryer basket and cook at 350°F for 10 minutes.
3. Serve and enjoy.

Brown Sugar Baked Apples

Servings: 4 | Cooking Time: 15 Minutes

Ingredients:

- 3 Small tart apples, preferably McIntosh
- 4 tablespoons (¼ cup/½ stick) Butter
- 6 tablespoons Light brown sugar
- Ground cinnamon
- Table salt

Directions:

1. Preheat the air fryer to 400°F.
2. Stem the apples, then cut them in half through their "equators". Use a melon baller to core the apples, taking care not to break through the flesh and skin at any point but creating a little well in the center of each half.
3. When the machine is at temperature, remove the basket and set it on a heat-safe work surface. Set the apple halves cut side up in the basket with as much air space between them as possible. Even a fraction of an inch will work. Drop 2 teaspoons of butter into the well in the center of each apple half. Sprinkle each half with 1 tablespoon brown sugar and a pinch each ground cinnamon and table salt.
4. Return the basket to the machine. Air-fry undisturbed for 15 minutes, or until the apple halves have softened and the brown sugar has caramelized.
5. Use a nonstick-safe spatula to transfer the apple halves cut side up to a wire rack. Cool for at least 10 minutes before serving, or serve at room temperature.

Brown Sugar Cookies

Servings:9 | Cooking Time: 27 Minutes

Ingredients:

- 4 tablespoons salted butter, melted
- ⅓ cup granular brown erythritol
- 1 large egg
- ½ teaspoon vanilla extract
- 1 cup blanched finely ground almond flour
- ½ teaspoon baking powder

Directions:

1. In a large bowl, whisk together butter, erythritol, egg, and vanilla. Add flour and baking powder, and stir until combined.
2. Separate dough into nine pieces and roll into balls, about 2 tablespoons each.
3. Cut three pieces of parchment paper to fit your air fryer basket and place three cookies on each ungreased piece. Place one piece of parchment into air fryer basket. Adjust the temperature to 300°F and set the timer for 9 minutes. Edges of cookies will be browned when done. Repeat with remaining cookies. Serve warm.

Custard

Servings: 4 | Cooking Time: 45 Minutes

Ingredients:

- 2 cups whole milk
- 2 eggs
- ¼ cup sugar
- ⅛ teaspoon salt
- ¼ teaspoon vanilla
- cooking spray
- ⅛ teaspoon nutmeg

Directions:

1. In a blender, process milk, egg, sugar, salt, and vanilla until smooth.
2. Spray a 6 x 6-inch baking pan with nonstick spray and pour the custard into it.
3. Cook at 300°F for 45 minutes. Custard is done when the center sets.
4. Sprinkle top with the nutmeg.
5. Allow custard to cool slightly.
6. Serve it warm, at room temperature, or chilled.

Glazed Donuts

Servings: 2 – 4 | Cooking Time: 25 Minutes

Ingredients:

- 1 can [8 oz.] refrigerated croissant dough
- Cooking spray
- 1 can [16 oz.] vanilla frosting

Directions:

1. Cut the croissant dough into 1-inch-round slices. Make a hole in the center of each one to create a donut.
2. Put the donuts in the Air Fryer basket, taking care not to overlap any, and spritz with cooking spray. You may need to cook everything in multiple batches.
3. Cook at 400°F for 2 minutes. Turn the donuts over and cook for another 3 minutes.
4. Place the rolls on a paper plate.
5. Microwave a half-cup of frosting for 30 seconds and pour a drizzling of the frosting over the donuts before serving.

Cranberry Jam

Servings: 8 | Cooking Time: 20 Minutes

Ingredients:

- 2 pounds cranberries
- 4 ounces black currant
- 2 pounds sugar
- Zest of 1 lime
- 3 tablespoons water

Directions:

1. In a pan that fits your air fryer, add all the ingredients and stir.
2. Place the pan in the fryer and cook at 360°F for 20 minutes.
3. Stir the jam well, divide into cups, refrigerate, and serve cold.

Cinnamon Pretzels

Servings:6 | Cooking Time: 10 Minutes

Ingredients:

- 1½ cups shredded mozzarella cheese
- 1 cup blanched finely ground almond flour
- 2 tablespoons salted butter, melted, divided
- ¼ cup granular erythritol, divided
- 1 teaspoon ground cinnamon

Directions:

1. Place mozzarella, flour, 1 tablespoon butter, and 2 tablespoons erythritol in a large microwave-safe bowl. Microwave on high 45 seconds, then stir with a fork until a smooth dough ball forms.
2. Separate dough into six equal sections. Gently roll each section into a 12" rope, then fold into a pretzel shape.
3. Place pretzels into ungreased air fryer basket. Adjust the temperature to 370°F and set the timer for 8 minutes, turning pretzels halfway through cooking.
4. In a small bowl, combine remaining butter, remaining erythritol, and cinnamon. Brush ½ mixture on both sides of pretzels.
5. Place pretzels back into air fryer and cook an additional 2 minutes at 370°F.
6. Transfer pretzels to a large plate. Brush on both sides with remaining butter mixture, then let cool 5 minutes before serving.

Pineapple Sticks

Servings: 4 | Cooking Time: 20 Minutes

Ingredients:

- ½ fresh pineapple, cut into sticks
- ¼ cup desiccated coconut

Directions:

1. Pre-heat the Air Fryer to 400°F.
2. Coat the pineapple sticks in the desiccated coconut and put each one in the Air Fryer basket.
3. Air fry for 10 minutes.

Mini Crustless Peanut Butter Cheesecake

Servings:2 | Cooking Time: 10 Minutes

Ingredients:

- 4 ounces cream cheese, softened
- 2 tablespoons confectioners' erythritol
- 1 tablespoon all-natural, no-sugar-added peanut butter
- ½ teaspoon vanilla extract
- 1 large egg, whisked

Directions:

1. In a medium bowl, mix cream cheese and erythritol until smooth. Add peanut butter and vanilla, mixing until smooth. Add egg and stir just until combined.
2. Spoon mixture into an ungreased 4" springform nonstick pan and place into air fryer basket. Adjust the temperature to 300°F and set the timer for 10 minutes. Edges will be firm, but center will be mostly set with only a small amount of jiggle when done.
3. Let pan cool at room temperature 30 minutes, cover with plastic wrap, then place into refrigerator at least 2 hours. Serve chilled.

Delicious Vanilla Custard

Servings: 2 | Cooking Time: 20 Minutes

Ingredients:

- 5 eggs
- 2 tbsp swerve
- 1 tsp vanilla
- ½ cup unsweetened almond milk
- ½ cup cream cheese

Directions:

1. Add eggs in a bowl and beat using a hand mixer.
2. Add cream cheese, sweetener, vanilla, and almond milk and beat for 2 minutes more.
3. Spray two ramekins with cooking spray.
4. Pour batter into the prepared ramekins.
5. Preheat the air fryer to 350°F.
6. Place ramekins into the air fryer and cook for 20 minutes.
7. Serve and enjoy.

Cocoa Spread

Servings: 4 | Cooking Time: 5 Minutes

Ingredients:

- 2 oz walnuts, chopped
- 5 teaspoons coconut oil
- ½ teaspoon vanilla extract
- 1 tablespoon Erythritol
- 1 teaspoon of cocoa powder

Directions:

1. Preheat the air fryer to 350°F. Put the walnuts in the mason jar. Add coconut oil, vanilla extract, Erythritol, and cocoa powder. Stir the mixture until smooth with the help of the spoon. Then place the mason jar with Nutella in the preheated air fryer and cook it for 5 minutes. Stir Nutella before serving.

Fried Banana S'mores

Servings: 4 | Cooking Time: 6 Minutes

Ingredients:

- 4 bananas
- 3 tablespoons mini semi-sweet chocolate chips
- 3 tablespoons mini peanut butter chips
- 3 tablespoons mini marshmallows
- 3 tablespoons graham cracker cereal

Directions:

1. Preheat the air fryer to 400°F.
2. Slice into the un-peeled bananas lengthwise along the inside of the curve, but do not slice through the bottom of the peel. Open the banana slightly to form a pocket.
3. Fill each pocket with chocolate chips, peanut butter chips and marshmallows. Poke the graham cracker cereal into the filling.
4. Place the bananas in the air fryer basket, resting them on the side of the basket and each other to keep them upright with the filling facing up. Air-fry for 6 minutes, or until the bananas are soft to the touch, the peels have blackened and the chocolate and marshmallows have melted and toasted.
5. Let them cool for a couple of minutes and then simply serve with a spoon to scoop out the filling.

D

E

T

V

W

Y

Z

Made in the USA
Las Vegas, NV
11 January 2024

84191807R00057